Superwoman Myths

Break the Rules of Silence and Speak UP your Truth!

Compiled by Kristy-Lea Tritz

Co-Authored with:

Angela Del Bianco

Ashley Blair Hill

Autumne Stirling

Ayesha Hilton

Barb Heite

Dr.Biljana Karamehmedovic

Charlene Schmidt

Christine Merritt

Cindy Leavitt

Debbie Franklin

Eleni Szemeti

Janiece Montano

Jeanette MacDonald

Jeannine Riant

Jenni Ryan

Jennifer Gardner

Jenny Call

Jerri Eddington

Karen Packwood

Kris McLeod

Kylie Firns

Laura Probert

Lauren King

Lisa McAdams

Rebecca Thompson

Samantha Dobler

Shannon Riley

Tandy Elisala

Tara-Lee York

Ty Will

and Vanessa Higgins

Empower and Inspire Publishing

www.empowerandinspirepublising.com

contact@empowerandinspirepublishing.com

ISBN: — 13: 978-0-9936829-1-9

Interior Layout: Kristy-Lea Tritz

Book Cover: Csernik Elod

Published in: Canada, USA, UK, Australia

Dedication

This book is dedicated to those children lost too soon in life.

If you have lost a child too soon we dedicate this book to you in memory of your child. We would like to especially dedicate in memory of:

Xavier Grey Thompson

April 4, 2014

Katelyn Marie (Leavitt) Perkins

April 15, 1993 - October 30, 2014

Gratitude

"To be grateful is to hold a diamond of change in your hand daily."~Kristy-Lea Tritz

Creating a space in your heart for gratitude, even when things seem to be doom and gloom in your life, is truly the only way in which to see the sparkle life has to offer. Life is not always easy, this is true, but it can be what you decide it will be. We get to choose to live in a space of positivity or a space of negativity. We are not stuck someplace because of our age, race, gender, or anything else. Life is a blessing, and we get to choose where our life journey will take us despite any circumstances or situations we may experience.

Gratitude is not something I take lightly in my life. I treasure each moment of every day. Embrace a life of gratitude. Learn from the lessons that surround you. Take up those lessons and touch other lives!

My Gratitude

I am grateful for the opportunity and freedom to practice my faith, to believe in God, and to be a Christian. I am grateful for this because without it, I would not be where I am today. I would not have the courage to write a chapter in this book if it was not for my faith, for it allowed me to break through the bonds of fear. I thank God for the gifts He has given me to share through writing, speaking, and coaching.

I am grateful for my son, Jacob. I hug him a little longer, hold his hand a little tighter, and love him a little more deeply each day because I am grateful for his joyous presence in my life. He is the ray of sunshine on a cloudy day. Thank you for always bringing smiles and hugs into my life. I love you!

I am grateful for my husband, Sebastien, who has challenged me to be the best woman I can. Without him and the challenges we have faced together, I would not have stepped out of my comfort zones. I have learned that even when your marriage has challenges, you can choose to take them as opportunities to learn and grow, or you can allow them to consume you. He is my love, my friend, and most of all, my life journey partner. Marriage is a journey filled with unbelievable obstacles at times, but love truly can conquer all when both people choose to change their life journey together. Through the process of compiling this book and creating my programs, he has been a solid rock, and for this I will be eternally grateful. Thanks for being there through this journey and for keeping me in a place of creative solitude, for loving me for me, and for being strong. I love you!

I am grateful for my daddy, Nicolas, who taught me what love is. I remember clearly standing at my window as he drove away for work, crying because I missed him. The love he shines forth is unlike any other I have experienced in my life. I am grateful for this amazing gift he has passed on to me to truly love my fellow men and women for who they are. Dad, you are my best friend. Thank you for always listening with a loving ear. I love you!

I am grateful for my mom, Debra, who taught me what it was to be a woman of God and what it meant to love your spouse. She has been my level head when I felt I could no longer go on. Mom, you are my rock. Thanks for always being my calming place when my head was spinning in thoughts. I love you!

I am grateful for my sisters, Nicole, Melissa, and Jennifer, who have been with me during the whole journey of my life. You have always been there no matter how near or far we are from each other, and I can always feel your love. Thank you for being light when I was in darkness and for always making me laugh. No love is like sister love! I love you all!

I am grateful for all the co-authors who joined me on this journey, and who—as you will see in the chapters you read—were real, raw, and genuine so that others could find hope and healing in their own lives. Together we can! It is when we are alone that we drown. Thank you for all your hard work in writing your chapters, for the tears we shared together, and for your friendship. I will forever hold a special place in my heart for each one of you!

Gratefulness is a gift to be treasured and shared. I hope that as you read each chapter contained in this book, you find even more ways to be grateful in your own life. I pray you will find inspiration in the words shared on the following pages and that as you go forth from this moment, you take time every day to dwell on the things that create gratefulness for you. Sending each one of you heart hugs!

Much joy and love, Kristy-Lea Tritz

Forward

When I was twenty-three years old, I started my first business. I had no business experience, no business training, and was convinced I would be a stay-at-home mom and never work again once I had children.

But God definitely has a plan for us. Sometimes He gives us trials to learn from, and sometimes He gives us blessings to learn from. He blessed me with really good babies, babies that just sit there and look at you. I thought to myself, "I love that baby more than life itself, but I am bored out of my mind."

And that is when I started my first business. Most of us who are DO-ers, and especially those of us who have children, think we need to overcome our God-given personalities and be calm, quiet, and lovely. We tell ourselves we need to slow down and keep the pace of the people around us. We think we need to become BE-ers. I finally got the relief I was looking for when I realized—there is nothing wrong with being who you are created to be!

God made you a DO-er because you have something to DO!

A dear friend, a woman whom I admired and looked up to, came over to chat one day. She warned me, "Kim, you are out of alignment. It is fine to have some ambition, but you have too much." And then she said the one sentence that would ring in my ears, haunting me for the next seven years. "A mom can do small things, but you can't do big things."

I played in that space for seven years, but God is good. I grew my first business—tutoring—to employ about thirty people and in the meantime, I started another business almost every two years thereafter. I started a property management business, a personal training business, and an image consulting business.

I began getting recruited from other corporations and companies to join their teams. One day, a corporate woman whom I greatly respected came to my home office and said to me, "You are very capable. You have a lot of talent. You can do anything you want to do. But what is it that you want?"

I sat there completely stumped. I didn't know. I could have spouted off some canned interview answers, but the truth is I didn't know. And there is a reason I didn't know what I wanted. Follow this next thought carefully: The reason I didn't know what I wanted is because I didn't dare to think big enough. What my soul was crying out for was bigger than what my logical mind could accept.

I told her the truth. I had the skills of an entrepreneur, but I hadn't given myself permission to reach for my potential. I hadn't given myself permission to play BIG.

I turned down the offers to work with all the companies, sold all of my previous businesses, and started my own consulting firm. After four years, I have never felt more sure of my path, more inspired in what I do, or more grateful to serve. I teach women (and a few brave men) how to systematize, structure, and organize their work so they can grow their businesses to their potential. I lead national business-intensive retreats, where entrepreneurs learn the unsexy truth of how to grow successful businesses.

Kim Flynn

Introduction

"Many live a superwoman-myth-filled life. It is those who bust through them, speak truth, and no longer live in silence who make an impact on the world!" ~Kristy-Lea Tritz

Superwoman myths are real and lived by women all over the globe. These myths can take over the life you yearn to live in your heart and replace them with symptoms such as feelings of loneliness, despair, unhappiness, depression, and so many more. Often it takes us hitting the bottom or getting really fed up with our current situation to even recognize that we have been living in the shadows of Superwoman Myths.

Society has called women to be many things, to take on many roles, to consume thoughts and images of what we are "supposed" to be like, but in truth, these only cause damage to the very heart of a woman—the place where her light can shine the greatest.

How do you know if you live by these Superwoman Myths? What are they? This book will uncover for you, through the stories of women, what some of these myths can look like in our daily life and what happens when you speak up in truth and really live instead of being held captive by silence.

Here are the top ten Superwoman Myths women can identify with quite quickly in their lives and even in the lives of other women they come into contact with.

Top Ten Superwoman Myths

1. Women shouldn't complain; they should be able to fix anything or anyone.

2. Women shouldn't ask for help, they shouldn't take days off for themselves.

3. Women shouldn't be so emotional; they shouldn't get angry.

4. Women should be silent and not speak up when wronged.

5. Women should be able to juggle multiple roles without complaint.

6. Women shouldn't follow their hearts or listen to their instinctual voices.

7. Women can't be successful in business if they are mothers.

8. Women can't make great incomes doing what they love.

9. Women should be able to handle everything.

10. Women are naturally-born mothers and/or motherhood comes naturally.

It is the goal of this book to help you bust through your own Superwoman Myths so that you can truly experience life, discover who you are, and really embrace and listen to your heart. As you read through each chapter, you will be given an inside look at how some of these myths have impacted the lives of the women who share their stories with you and how they were able to overcome!

Let's bust down the doors of silence together, no longer living our Superwoman Myths but living in truth!

Letter from the Compiler

"The beginning is where all things start. Create beginnings every day of your life!" ~Kristy-Lea Tritz

Every book, every journey, has a starting place. The beginning can be a great blossom of color into your life, or at times, it may be that start of darkness creeping in. Life takes us on many journeys, some more pleasant than others. The good news is that the beginning of the journey is not the end.

In between the beginning and the end is choice. Choice is one of those things that creates for you either a landing ground of perseverance or an attitude of giving up. It can create for you a blanket of happiness or pain. The greatest news of all is that no matter where we begin, it is the in-between that counts the most.

This book is about that in-between, about the choices made that either bring further pain or open up the floodgates of joy! There is no end without a beginning and there is no beginning without an end. Together, through each chapter of this book, we will journey with each author into their middle—their choice to overcome.

As I reflect on the journey of compiling this book, I see how much the Superwoman Myth played out in the roles of wife, mother, daughter, sister. Most importantly, I see how much it changed my life just as "me."

Often times I have lived a superwoman myth life. I have worn that mask of happiness even when I was feeling the deepest pain. I felt I had to be everything to everyone and that their health, joy, and wellness hinged on my shoulders.

Compiling this book opened my eyes even further to what living a superwoman myth life does to you as a person. It can take over and make you feel lost and lonely. Breaking free from those daily Superwoman Myths truly sets you free to experience life. When I moved from living a Superwoman Myth life into truly living, I came alive.

It is my hope that as you read this book you will be set free from your own Superwoman Myths, no longer live in silence, and speak UP your truth. For change does not occur unless you take a step forward in the right direction.

CONTENTS

Kristy-Lea Tritz

Kristy-Lea Tritz is an internationally best-selling author, heart-centered woman's empowerment coach, podcast host, online TV show host and speaker.

She began her journey to become a heart-centered woman's empowerment coach out of her own struggles in life. She created and facilitates the "Get to the Heart of the Matter" programs.

Kristy-Lea is also the author of *Coldilocks and the Three Polar Bears*, a children's book she wrote when she was just fifteen years old. It has always been a dream of Kristy-Lea's to publish her books, and now that her dream is becoming a reality, she says her life is filled with more passion to write!

Kristy-Lea is a creative individual who enjoys the great outdoors.

> **www.empowerandinspirepublishing.com**
> **www.gettotheheartofthematter.ca**
> **www.kristyleatritz.com**
> **kristylea@superwomanmyths.com**
> **www.facebook.com/gettotheheartofthematter**
> **twitter.com/kristyleatritz**
> **youtube.com/kristyleatritz**
> **google.com/+KristyLeaTritzwrites**
> **ca.linkedin.com/in/kristyleatritz**

COMPILED by **KRISTY-LEA TRITZ**

Chapter 1

BUILDING A TOWER OF POSITIVITY: DESPITE THE NEGATIVE EFFECTS OF SPOUSAL ADDICTION

Kristy-Lea Tritz

The box was like any other box. It had four sides and was a cover for something. The pictures on the box, however, were unlike any other I had ever seen.

Nude people splashed across the glossy cover. *How disturbing*, I thought to myself, as my heart sank. I suddenly felt sick to my stomach. I had no idea what I was looking at as I looked at the images on the box. This was my first exposure to such raw, rude material. I was quickly going to find out the impact this small box would have on my life— my happily ever after.

In public, we were the lovey-dovey couple. We held hands, snuck in kisses, and were close. Like one of those couples I found myself looking at before I was married— wishing, hoping that someday I would marry someone like that.

At home, however, something was tearing us apart from the inside out. My husband was hiding a dark secret. He had an addiction to pornography.

I just wanted to lie down and leave the world behind. I couldn't stand the pain that surrounded my life. Permanently plastered to my face was the hide-it-all smile— something I had mastered. If someone had asked me what was wrong, I would have broken apart right before their eyes. I couldn't do that. I couldn't let someone see the pain I was hiding inside!

I was in total despair, feeling the fear of rejection—as if there were something wrong with me. How unloved I felt in my marriage. I would roll over most nights feeling like I was living hell here on Earth. I would cry myself to sleep. I hid behind the mask of a smile.

I am one of those women who love to love. I love deeply, I feel deeply, and I cherish deeply. Here lay beside me someone I was called to love, and I felt the furthest thing coming from them. I hurt deeper than I had ever before. Even more, honestly, than I had when I was raped and assaulted. This was someone I loved. Someone who was supposed to love me. What was I supposed to do?

Loneliness took over and darkness consumed me. The light I once had seemed to vanish.

It was after the death of a very special aunt, just a short while after losing my Oma, that I lost myself yet again. The first time had happened after a four-year abusive relationship. Here I was again unable to grieve the loss, finding myself waking up and not wanting to face the day. Just wishing it would come to an end so I could go back to sleep. Somehow stop the pain if but for a moment. I was ALONE! I held back tears every waking moment. I felt tortured and imprisoned in my marriage and my life!

The darkest hour rose. I was lost, wandering in a wilderness I couldn't find my way through. The more I wandered, the more lost I became. I would look in the mirror and could not recognize the woman staring back at me. Who was she? Was there hope for her anymore? Would she be lost forever? She hid a secret that wasn't even her own. She lived in turmoil over something she couldn't control.

I found myself struggling more and more, drawn in by the words of other men's sultry tongues spewing comments of praises and uplifting words. It made me feel special and beautiful. It was like a seductive rope. It was dangerous.

I felt closed off. I shut down, like I used to, and went someplace else in my head. I dissociated with the painful world that surrounded me. I felt worthless to my own husband. I hated the control his addiction had over me, over our family. I felt our marriage didn't matter. I didn't matter! This scared me because I knew what life was like when I withdrew to the point of complete separation.

It was awfully quiet downstairs. I had that feeling again something was wrong in the depths of me when I caught him watching pornography! I was furious! I came clean with him about what was happening inside me. I told him everything. I was raw and real and spilled everything I had been holding within me.

He began to cry, which I had only seen once before in our ten-year relationship. He stood there in shock at how deeply I was hurt. I told him how I had begun losing my faith in God and that if something didn't change, I would have to leave for my soul's sake.

Looking in my eyes, tears rolling down his cheeks, he said, "Kristy-Lea, I didn't know it was this bad for you. I'm so sorry I hurt you like that. I will do what it takes! This time, I promise to do whatever it takes to make this right. I don't want to be enslaved to this addiction anymore. I just don't know how to overcome it."

I had heard those words before. How was I supposed to believe him when everything behind my back was one lie covered by another lie? This was his last chance to be honest with me and show me he was willing to do whatever it took to save our marriage. I knew inside that if he didn't, I would have to move forward in life without him. I couldn't live in hell anymore! I wanted to live LIFE!

I still had a choice. It was either exude positivity or dwell in the negativity. My husband's addiction was not going to rule my life any longer. I had made mistakes, we both had, but I was going to rise up out of the ashes and stand victorious no matter what!

Somewhere inside, I knew that my faith and God were stronger than anything this world could throw at me. My heart was battered and bruised, but a light of hope still flickered within my soul. Christ's promises echoed through every fiber of my being. "I will never leave you nor forsake you. I know well the plans I have for you!"

I held onto these promises. They were my ray of sunshine within the darkness. There were times when I wanted to leave, not because I didn't love him, but because having my heart ripped apart daily was exhausting. The feelings of loneliness, isolation, rejection, feeling unattractive and unloved were overwhelming.

Ultimately, I loved my husband beyond expressive words. I could see the man within! Every day I prayed. It was the only thing I knew how to do that didn't bring more pain, but it was only a fraction of the pain in the equation. He too was suffering, maybe even deeper than I was.

He was going to have to crawl out of the depths of addiction and only he could do it!

This was over my head, I knew that. I knew God had a greater plan for our marriage than pain and suffering! I read every book, every article, and anything I could get my hands on. I don't think anything in the world could've prepared me for the journey over these ten years.

I knew I needed to start healing the wounds this situation had created within me. I needed to continue to grow as a person and find myself again. I could only change ME!

I looked for support groups for women with husbands like mine, but to no avail. And in that moment, I knew I was called to be a beacon of hope to other wives who suffered in silence. It's a difficult place to be when you feel helpless to change a situation, when loneliness and feelings of being unloved consume you.

Through all of it, I came to an even deeper understanding of how important it was to BE change, rather than trying to change others. I learned how important it was to renew myself from the inside out. I couldn't let this addiction overtake me and my marriage!

You are not alone. Yes, YOU, reading this. There is hope, even when it feels like all hope is lost. You can feel whole again. There *is* a better life for you...

I know what it's like to have your voice silenced. It has driven me to write this chapter and to help other women whose voices have been silenced to find a way through the prison of silence into the freedom of sharing their voices even when it seems impossible. Without going through what

I have, I wouldn't be blessed to work with women and see them overcome so many obstacles in their lives. I encourage you, break the silence, speak UP your truth and be set FREE!

Angela Del Bianco

Angela Del Bianco is a life and business coach, entrepreneur, and author. Born in Australia to a Serbian father and German mother, Angela and her four siblings were ostracized growing up because they were poor and spoke little English. Angela overcame her language barriers to become a teacher, specializing in English as a second language. She has taught a range of motivational and inspirational courses and won awards for her teaching style. Angela and her husband run a whale watching company on Australia's Gold Coast. She is the mother of two gorgeous grownup children.

COMPILED by **KRISTY-LEA TRITZ**

Chapter 2

YOU ARE THE AUTHOR OF YOUR LIFE

Angela Del Bianco

"In the long run, we shape our lives, and we shape ourselves. The process never ends until we die and the choices we make are ultimately our responsibility." ~ Eleanor Roosevelt

I was born in Islington, New South Wales, Australia, into a European family (Serbian father and German mother). Not a good mix. Their fiery temperaments created an explosive environment. They fought like cats and dogs. Growing up wasn't all roses. As the second oldest of five siblings, I always felt I had to protect and look after the others—like a leader.

We suffered physical abuse and wore bruises throughout most of our childhood. Papa's way of understanding how to raise children was to beat them. As punishment once, Papa placed some stones on a concrete floor and made me kneel on them for what seemed like eternity. The physical pain was excruciating. He constantly whipped me and my siblings across our legs and backs with what looked like a solid rubber hose. I'm not sure why, but my mother seemed to turn a blind eye to Papa beating us.

Papa was a soldier during World War II, and I think that had a big effect on him. He was high up in the ranks, a captain or something, and I'm sure he had to deal with a lot of traumatic experiences. He never shared any of his past with us. We never even met his family. It felt as if he was ashamed. Being a soldier was no excuse, though, for the harshness that was carried out on me as a child.

Mother and Papa fought frequently. I had this innate need to protect my siblings. I would gather them together and hide in the back garage that was Papa's workshop. It was an amazing experience for me to protect my siblings. I had a great imagination. I was a bit of a storyteller.

I would tell them I had a magic wand and make biscuits appear as I would yell, "Abracadabra!" I was clever and took biscuits from the kitchen, pretending to produce my magic wand, and from nowhere, biscuits appeared much to the great surprise of my siblings. They really believed it! My magic wand and stories calmed us all down. Those times were magical for all of us just escaping the sounds of fighting parents.

Born into a European family in the 1950s was not easy going. We were poor and constantly reminded that we were "wogs"—a racial term used to identify immigrants from Europe. I remember feeling ashamed and different from peers.

It didn't get any easier from kindergarten to high school. Fellow students were overly rude, insulting, and very degrading towards me and my siblings. I recall being in the lunch shed at school, which I dreaded. I would open up my lunchbox and the smell of liverwurst or salami sandwiches filled the air. "What's that smell?" the kids would ask. And I would shut my lunchbox immediately. I just wished my mum would make me jam sandwiches.

My first day of high school was embarrassing. We couldn't even afford a uniform! I felt so humiliated. I liked school but it was a struggle just keeping up. The language spoken at home was a mix between English and German, thus my English was very limited. And I was behind in my studies before classes even started. I had no support at home, either. I felt lonely. It took me a long time to master English. It made me feel like I wasn't good enough. All my school reports stated I was an introvert. That had a negative impact on my self-esteem. A sense of unworthiness stayed with me for many years.

One of my dreams was to become a teacher; I knew I was a natural encourager. And I knew what it was like being a child that had to go without and was picked on and ridiculed. I wanted to help others so they didn't have to feel what I had felt. Unfortunately, the school counsellor shot my dreams to pieces when she said my grades were too low to be a teacher. I was absolutely devastated. In one insignificant moment for the counsellor, my dream to teach, my hopes, and my confidence were extinguished.

The fighting at home boiled over one too many times, and when I was sixteen Mother left Papa. With only three garbage bags full of our possessions, we headed for Sydney by train. The Salvation Army came to our rescue. They provided us with shelter, food, and accommodation upon our arrival. My mother, at the age of fifty, took a job as a cleaner at the children's hospital to pay rent and feed us. We lived in a house with twelve rooms, occupied by us and other tenants. The worst part was sharing the one bathroom between all the tenants, but we seemed to make do.

I found myself a job so I could help my mother out

financially. My boss gave me a compliment that I will remember forever –"You have such a beautiful smile when greeting customers." One of his clients mentioned to him, "Do you pay your receptionist extra money for that smiling face?"

It changed my life and the way in which I viewed myself. I had a renewed sense of confidence and self-respect. This gave me a platform to take ownership of my destiny; it had an amazing impact on my life—a path to realizing my goals, aspirations, and dreams.

I made up my school failures by becoming a lifelong learner. The dictionary became my best friend! I attended TAFE to improve my English and undertook various courses, including shorthand and office procedures, to increase my working skills. I took personal development courses to gain self-confidence and be able to speak more confidently. I was on fire with learning!

The turning point in my life came when I was twenty-one years old. I received a phone call to enter the Miss Australia Quest. I sincerely believed they had the wrong number, so I hung up. They phoned again, and the organization assured me they wanted to speak with me! It was not a beauty pageant, but instead they were raising money towards The Spastic Centre, now known as the Cerebral Palsy Alliance.

When I look back, as I got on stage to thank everyone for all their efforts and contributions towards The Spastic Centre, I realize how this played a major role in increasing my confidence level. It seemed natural at the time, natural to thank people for their incredible support.

My confidence grew over the years, and my dream of

becoming a teacher became a reality! I graduated at the age of forty-seven from the University of Newcastle (NSW) in adult educational studies. My first teaching position was at a private business college, where I taught business studies, communication, and personal development. From there, I developed motivational courses and taught them at evening college. I was awarded Tutor of the Year—the biggest surprise of my life! I'm so glad I kept the vision alive of becoming a teacher, changing many lives along the way.

I later qualified to teach English to foreign students, or TESOL. As soon as I finished the course, my phone rang. I was asked if I would take on a six-month assignment in China. I always wanted to go to China, ever since I was a kid, after I saw the movie, *The Inn of the Sixth Happiness*, starring Ingrid Bergman. Another dream was coming true!

I taught for six months at the China Hong Kong English School in Jiangmen, Guangzhou—a private boarding school for eight hundred students. This experience was incredible. Teaching was so much fun! The students looked at me as their mum. During my time in China, I felt like a princess. Meals were cooked for me, and cleaners took care of my room. Gone was the childhood poverty I once lived in. It was replaced with a dream life.

Returning to Australia, I commenced teaching English at language schools after my experience in China. This has become my real passion. It came naturally to me, as I knew firsthand how difficult it was for me growing up with a language barrier—just like these students.

Destiny is in your hands. Believe, and you will achieve.

Overcoming adversity in life gives us the strength to

grow. The lessons we learn form the backbone of who we are today. How you respond/react to situations, no matter how tough, makes you the author of your life.

I would like to leave you with my favourite saying that has guided me though the rough times: "Your future will look bright if your attitude is right!"

Ashley Blair Hill

Ashley Blair Hill earned her bachelor's degree in journalism and mass communications from the University of South Carolina, and her master's degree in management and leadership from Webster University.

Ashley is the author of *The Art of the Spectrum* and is currently working on a series of children's book based on faith and victory.

She's an inspirational writer and life coach, specializing in spiritual growth and evolution. She has spent the last few years mentoring parents and families who are striving to overcome autism challenges and the shadows of their past.

COMPILED by **KRISTY-LEA TRITZ**

Chapter 3

LET THE WALLS OF JERICHO FALL: OVERCOMING AUTISM

Ashley Blair Hill

Just twenty-six and pregnant. My husband and I were very excited, even though this pregnancy was unexpected. I was experiencing sharp pains in my abdomen region and I knew there was a problem.

When we went in for the ultrasound, the tech said to me, "Here is your baby," and I got excited. Then she proceeded to say, "Here is your other baby." I was like *what? The other baby?*

I was having twins. I felt honoured to be carrying not one but two babies. My husband and I were so excited and started planning for our boy and girl. It was time to do the blue and pink thing. My pregnancy after this incident was perfect, and I didn't have any further scares or issues.

My twins' development was beautiful—up until they were about nine months old. Watching my two children interact and start the babbling phase of saying "ma-ma" and "da-da," I knew right away that something was wrong.

My son was developing at normal rate but not my daughter. She would only say *mama* and nothing else. I began to pay very close attention to her. I noticed that when she was crawling, she was dragging one leg on the floor. Her attention was also not there. She wouldn't notice noises and sounds. Looking at my beautiful child, I knew something was different and wasn't quite right.

Looking back into my childhood, I remembered something. It was in a paper I had written in high school about autism. I was sixteen years old. Our teacher told us to pick a topic to research and write on. I chose autism. I was so drawn to the topic that I checked out every book I could find from the library. My teacher told me it was the best paper she had read from a junior in high school. Little did I know the impact that writing that paper would have on my life ten years later as I watched my daughter grow.

God had brought the memory of this paper to my mind. He told me what I was seeing was something I had read before. It was something I had heard before. It was autism. I knew it!

I had to look deeper into it and that is exactly what I did. I reached out to resources I had in the autism community. I found comfort there by sharing what was going on and the signs and symptoms I was seeing. They confirmed for me that I should have her tested.

It was frustrating for me. As a mother, I wanted my child to be perfect and carefree. I didn't want anything to be wrong with her. I felt like it was my fault that she was struggling like this. I began to blame myself. I wanted to know what it was I had done wrong! Was it because I got pregnant before I got married? I beat myself up trying to figure it out. And I was very angry with God.

I watched videos of other children and Googled autism. I identified my daughter with the images I saw and the things I read. By this point, she had stopped talking to us and stopped listening. We would call her name but she wouldn't answer. We thought maybe she just had a hearing problem; however, we found out that wasn't the case. This was another symptom of autism.

In addition to not paying attention to us and not talking, she would flap her hands uncontrollably, spin around in circles, and stack her toys. Her brother would try and play with her but she wouldn't respond. It was a very sad sight for me.

My son came into this world with someone and to watch her act like he didn't exist was very hurtful. She was the same toward her me and her father. We might have been in the same room as her, but there was no connection. It was very difficult.

I was so upset and hurt. I spent nights crying, blaming and pointing fingers. After this was over, God brought back to me how he had prepared me for this. He had chosen my daughter to come into my life with this affliction so I could show the world what happened when you applied the principles of faith and spoke into the atmosphere of someone's life. I was to use all I had learned as a little girl when I had to walk by faith. He wanted me to do the same for my daughter.

It was a hard pill to swallow. It was easier for me to do it for myself, but when I had to do it for my child, it was different. I had a lot more emotions attached to it. Why me? Why her? I realized it was up to me to fight for her life. God wanted me to step up to the plate, activate the principles of faith, and speak into the atmosphere of her life.

God told me he would show me what I would need to do

to bring forth healing in her life. He told me that if I did exactly what he would ask of me, she would be healed, and that by kindergarten, she would attend regular classes. I was given a very specific assignment.

In church one day, God spoke so loud to me that I couldn't even hear the pastor preaching! It was September, the month of harvest. For three days, I prepared myself for the journey I was about to go on. I was to start the process he requested of me on September 7 and end on the September 28. I got up every night at 3:00 a.m. and went into my child's room to pray with her.

At this point, I didn't know what he wanted me to pray. Oddly enough, there was a book I had never seen before on the night stand. I opened the book and found a prayer specific for autistic children. Indeed, he had provided the prayer.

I prayed into her ears so that her brain could process my words. I prayed for her mind. I prayed for her mouth. My prayers were that she would be able to hear the truth and what was being said to her, that she would be able to speak, and that her brain would process things properly. Taking her hands into mine, I would seal her tiny hands in my own and pray that she would stop the hand flapping.

Faithfully, I went in her room at 3:00 a.m. for those twenty-one days. It was difficult. I would wake up and see my husband beside me, sleeping peacefully. God would remind me in the difficulties that I had birthed her and she had a closeness with me she didn't have with anyone else.

Time passed, and slowly but surely, the symptoms of autism began to fall away from her. The hand flapping stopped. She began to speak more words. She went from having speech therapy to the therapist telling me she no longer needed it. She went from being in an autism spectrum classroom to being told she could no longer go because it was not the best place for her anymore.

She was moved into a mixed classroom—of kids with disabilities and without. There, she was also eventually told she no longer belonged. The miracle was happening and unfolding just as God had told me it would. Here she was at age four—ready for preschool, just about to go into kindergarten. God kept his promise—my little girl was going to go to a regular kindergarten. She was being healed!

The day I found out my child was going into the regular kindergarten program, I went home and cried on my husband's shoulder. He cried with me.

If you are a mother, or anyone else who has experience with children who have disabilities or difficulties, don't give up on them. I remember when my daughter would spin around in church, and I would take her and begin dancing with her, showing her that she didn't have to spin around in circles, that there were other things she could do. I called my journey my Jericho.

Even though you may be going through a Jericho experience, the walls can be broken down. You can turn everything around that was made to be bad and create good from it.

Autumne Stirling

Autumne Stirling is a social worker with a background in child protection, emergency room trauma, mental health, concurrent disorders, and chronic pain. She is a survivor of childhood trauma. She has struggled and subsequently learned to thrive with dissociative identity disorder, depression, anxiety, and self-harm. Her passion has now turned to writing, and this is her first publication. She intends to continue sharing her story, along with the various traditional and non-traditional forms of treatment she continues to use, in order to live an authentic, healing lifestyle.

> **www.strongwarriorhealing.com**
> **strongwarriorhealing@outlook.com**
> **www.facebook.com/strongwarriorhealing**
> **twitter.com/autumnestirling**
> **www.linkedin.com/pub/autumne-stirling/aa/300/158**

COMPILED by **KRISTY-LEA TRITZ**

Chapter 4

"UNDER CONSTRUCTION" SHIFTING BEYOND THE FRAGMENTS OF DISSOCIATIVE IDENTITY DISORDER

Autumne Stirling

I had a defining moment in my life. I felt, for the first time, what I now know to be trepidation. This premonition obsessively occupied my every waking hour and consequently became intertwined into the nightmares I had long since grown weary of.

My child's happiness, my very existence, and our world views depended on the forethought of my choices. This commitment was not a New Year's Eve resolution-type-decision that would hold strong for several weeks, subsequently followed by an instinctive retreat back into my relentless patterns of maladaptive behaviour. I needed to make an irrevocable choice to be healthy, harmonious, and healed—once and for all.

Defining "healthy" may be required here. My definition of healthy may vary slightly from yours. You see, I have the unique mental health diagnosis of Dissociative Identity Disorder (DID), which over time has led me to have significant self-destructive coping skills.

Officially diagnosed at age twenty-two, I have been thriving, struggling, coping, and reshaping my life with DID since I have been four years old. Having my exceptionality was the only way I knew how to live and had been my own personal version of normal since I was a little girl.

Normal living, at times, for me, has included random dissociation; self-harm, such as cutting, burning, and overdosing; depression that has its own breath, movement, and heartbeat; collapsing anxiety coupled with paralyzing panic attacks; insensitive suicide attempts; and personal moments of delicacy that have literally left me in anguish, isolated on the tear-saturated Earth, barren and fruitless.

Reconnecting my soul and restoring my balance was what I needed to be a consistent, compassionate, loving, tender mother and woman. Without doing this inescapable trauma work, I knew my demons would be chasing me for the rest of my life. My son deserved better. I deserved better.

Simply put, there was no possible way for me to remain in this state of vicious instability. With one swift, brave motion, I chose health and love and decided to dedicate myself to becoming centered, congruent, confident, capable, and committed. I was going to be everything they said I would never be.

I began a lifelong quest to discover who I truly was, and I was faithfully going to connect to all aspects of myself as I began to change and grow.

DID is a dissociative disorder that is best envisioned on a continuum. Everyone dissociates to some extent. Examples include daydreaming or driving a car and arriving at your destination without remembering the entire trip. DID is *oneself*, but with different fragments of oneself, without each fragment being aware or fully conscience of each other.

Dissociation is a process where one learns to cope by

distancing themselves psychologically and emotionally from a perceived or real danger, allowing survival of various life-threatening situations. This disorder can appear after repeated and prolonged experiences of childhood trauma that interrupt the progression of developmental milestones. It serves as a functional tool while one is experiencing chronic trauma. However, it inevitability becomes dysfunctional, unmanageable, and shameful as life progresses.

My trauma stems from exhaustive, remorseless, and diverse occurrences throughout my formative years—minimal validation, lack of attachment, the absence of consistency, and, unfortunately, suffering that resulted from growing up in our challenging psychiatric system.

Locating specialized therapy with a diagnosis of DID has proven to be quite precarious, frustrating, and segregating. Until four years ago, my journey has persistently highlighted the visibly inherent discrimination that can occur within segments in our psychiatric framework. I believe that there is an inaccurate perception of trauma and disassociate-based disorders rooted in misleading information driven from the media, the varying opinions of the psychiatric community, and from a small percentage of factitious cases of DID, that sadly generate more attention than the genuine ones.

Most—or all—individuals with DID do not transform into malicious "personalities" and execute murderous rampages. We do not hide out in old, sketchy motels on stretches of abandoned highways, clothed in hip waders, bearing a rusty axe, waiting to thump on your motel door.

In reality, having DID for me means, firstly, I am a person. I am also a woman, a mother, a girlfriend, and a friend. I have a master's degree. I am compassionate, genuine, and smart. I just happen to have eight other internal personalities with their own memories, feelings, and characteristics— none of whom have ever been violent, hostile, or arrested.

Just like others, I feel anger, shame, and pain. Happiness, empathy, and love are also feelings I am absolutely capable of enjoying. These are all completely humanistic qualities that make me just as trustworthy, lovable, and equal to everyone else.

As a trauma survivor, being authentically believed, validated, and respected is paramount. These values have helped me find the strength to love myself. My entire history has been germinated in lies, fear, suppressed anger, negativity, and confusion. I have learned that despite my complicated history, I am more than capable of personally owning my story, honouring my journey, and guiding my healing.

DID spoke an alien language I completely understood. It was naturally familiar and completely destructive. At first, I could not fathom how to replace the loathing and ingrained self-hatred I felt for myself. It whispered relentlessly. I needed to literally visualize a stop sign in my head, and replace the negative messages with beliefs of self-love in order to have a blooming, functional life.

To heal, I became desperate to master the vocabulary of wellness, seeking out traditional therapeutic avenues and numerous non-traditional healing activities. Ultimately, my combination of intensive professional treatment and my own longing for creative refuge made a remarkable difference in my recovery, allowing me to feel true happiness, love for myself, and subsequently, love for others.

My "defining moment" was not a catastrophic crisis situation. By reflecting, journaling, and having endless conversations, I have revealed that my moment was nothing more than a persistent and passionate thought of "what if?"

What if I chose recovery again and again, day after day, hour after hour, minute after minute?

What if I decided that guilt and shame were no longer going to be a part of my vocabulary?

What if I was determined to be self-loving yet unrelenting in my recovery?

What if I made frequent positive intentions?

What if I clearly manifested my thoughts, making them loving, kind, and gentle?

Motivating affirmations, positivity, and having clear directions and goals helped me move from a place of uninspiring self-deprivation to a place of active self-determination. In the end, it had to be me that craved this metamorphosis, moving myself from a scared, caged, and untrusting girl to a confident, independent, and empathetic woman. I found the courage to stand up and speak out.

The first time I spoke the reality of my adversity, I felt supported and strengthened. After all, with DID, the missing link simply comes down to connection. Having a loving and positive attachment to someone that is trustworthy and consistent leaves one feeling cared for, heard, believed, and above all else, safe.

I have learned some of my greatest lessons from peers in

patient treatment, most of who have also been disregarded and unloved.

I have learned that trust is possible, even though my past is smudged with thousands of reasons why I should run.

I have learned that recovery is what I chose it to be, and is what I will continue to make it for the rest of my life.

I have learned that trauma was hiding in every part of me. It lurked in my physical body, my mental cognition, my haunted heart and emotions, and in my inability to express myself. It concealed itself in my helpfulness, my need for perfection, and academic achievement. It created my own personal eclipse. All I saw was pain, darkness, heaviness, and weakness.

Trauma and its common companions of depression, self-hatred, shame, and blame all have their individual agendas. For me to recover, it became all about me winning. I was not going to let the people that had hurt me win. They were clearly not worth it.

Even though it took years, I now believe my truth. I can thrive, fully understanding that I will never be able to change them.

Since committing to a lifestyle completely focused on recovery, I have had several small relapses. This is natural, except I deal with these incidents completely differently. I now own my mistakes. I do not let them define me. I use my skills, love myself harder, and move on.

I am living in complete contrast to my previous existence. Life can be hard, but there is now purpose in the work, for the rewards are so much more extraordinary than the rejections.

Ayesha Hilton

Ayesha's superpower is helping women who have a big vision get it out of their heads and hearts and into reality fast. She is passionate about helping women grow their businesses so they can serve more people, doing what they love, while making a great income.

Ayesha's zone of genius and experience is in business strategy, marketing, and communications. She believes that gratitude is the key to creating the best life possible.

Ayesha lives in rural Victoria, Australia, with her husband, Nick, her two children, Grace and Spencer, their grandpa (Ayesha's dad), and their dog Holly.

www.ayeshahilton.com
www.facebook.com/ayeshahiltonpage
https://twitter.com/Ayesha_Hilton
au.linkedin.com/in/ayeshahilton

COMPILED by **KRISTY-LEA TRITZ**

Chapter 5

BEYOND THE FANTASY: HEALING FROM THE PAST TO CREATE LOVE IN THE CHAOS AND MESS OF REAL LIFE

Ayesha Hilton

I was one of those children who grew up feeling unlovable and unloved. Looking back now that I'm in my forties, I don't know if there was some truth to my feeling unloved, but it was the most defining thing about my childhood. It later played itself out in relationships and choices I made as an adult.

My mother was a single parent to four children—from three different fathers—all born within a four-year period. When she was in her early twenties in the 1970s, this was a shocking thing to be. Even the government had no experience supporting single parents, so they gave her the Widows' Pension. My dad was only nineteen when I was born, and he was mostly absent during my childhood.

I adored my three brothers. I was like a mother hen caring for her chicks. I was fiercely protective of them and took care of them when my mother was working or busy.

When I was about four, my mother was put in an awful situation, and to keep us safe, she surrendered my older brother to his father. It was the biggest sacrifice she would ever have to make. In hindsight, I know she did the right thing, but at the time, it was like the world had collapsed.

I can still remember that day vividly. I didn't realize that it would be a long time before I saw my brother again. He was like a hero to me. I adored him, and I would continue to miss him for the rest of my childhood. I'm not sure how long it was before I next saw my brother; it could have been a year or more.

He had changed. He was like a strange creature to me. He had a different haircut. He was dressed in military clothing. He lived in the middle of nowhere in a tent, living a life I couldn't understand. I knew him but didn't recognize him. I saw him about once a year after that. He grew up without a mother. I grew up without a father. It was a strange situation.

I watched families on TV, and in real life, with envy. I longed to have a normal family. I would visit friends and wish I were part of their family. I imagined myself being married in my mid-twenties and then having my first child at twenty-eight. That didn't happen for me, and my childhood experiences left me searching for love in all the wrong places.

When I was thirty-two, I met a man at a mediation course who would change my life. A few weeks after we had met, I was sitting in a toilet cubicle at work, holding a pregnancy test, staring at it in shock and amazement. The chances of me getting pregnant naturally due to medical issues were a million to one. Yet, there I was holding the proof in my hands, my period late, and apparently pregnant with a man I'd only just started dating.

Fast forward a few months, and I was living with the father of my miracle baby, trying hard to make a relationship with him work. But every day it became more apparent that this was not destined to be the family of my dreams.

I loved being pregnant. The wonder of creating a whole new life was amazing. But I was also miserable. I was pregnant with a man I didn't really know, and I wasn't sure I even wanted to have a relationship with him. But my yearning to create a stable family life made me try even harder to make it work. It was hard to accept that I was mirroring the life my mum had experienced.

The moment when you see your child for the first time is a memory that never leaves you. Covered in a film of vernix and blood, crying boldly, was my tiny daughter. I cried as I looked at her. It was the most powerful moment I had ever experienced. She was so lovely. I called her Grace Sophia— grace and wisdom. Grace's dad felt the intense emotion and was also crying.

I was totally involved in the most amazing love affair of my life. I was responsible for this new person, who struggled with feeding, who needed me more than anyone else ever had.

This was meant to be the happiest time of my life, but things were not going well in my relationship with Grace's dad. I put in so much effort for this vision of a perfect family so that I could give Grace what I'd never had, but I ended up sacrificing myself.

When Grace was just five weeks old, I realized that I had to let this fantasy go. This relationship was not going to work. I was going to lose myself even more than I had already. I could not sacrifice myself, or my beautiful daughter, for the sake of this dream of a normal family.

So I became a single parent with a five-week-old baby. I had no money and gratefully accepted government benefits. Somehow, I had recreated a version of my mother's life as a single parent. I wanted to give Grace the experience of what I imagined was a normal family, but sadly, I couldn't do it with her father. My dream was gone, but I still had hope and my love for my daughter.

Two long years later, I was living in a new town where I didn't know many people. I was in my mid-thirties, and my dream of having a normal family was still in my heart. I wanted to have someone special in my and Grace's life, and my biological clock was ticking loudly as I longed for another baby.

As a single parent working from home, I didn't meet any eligible men in my daily life. I created a profile on RSVP and went on a few dates but wasn't that interested in any of the men I dated. Just as I was about to give up on the whole online dating thing, I got an e-mail from a man named Nick. We started to communicate via e-mail and then later by phone.

A few months later, we finally met. We got along very well but I didn't see us being more than just friends. It was December, and we went to sing Christmas carols with my friends. Nick was a real gentleman, helping my friend carry chairs and food. She said to me, "He's a keeper." That was the night I decided I might just keep him.

We got married two years later. Even before we got married, Nick and I were trying to get pregnant. I had one child already, and for that I was thankful, but my longing for a second child was consuming. I just knew there was a soul destined to join our family. We tried for a long time, but eventually we decided we needed to take a break from trying to conceive.

A few weeks into our break, I was feeling unwell and took yet another pregnancy test, expecting it to be negative. To my delight, we were going to have a baby, and we couldn't keep it a secret from our family and friends. Even though the timing was terrible—we'd be having a harvest baby, which meant Nick would be busy harvesting the crops on our farm around end of the pregnancy—I didn't care.

Eight months passed quickly, and on Christmas day, I went into labor. In our living room, we had a white Christmas tree adorned with decorations and fairy lights. It's a pretty picture in my head that always reminds me of a magical time. I laboured all through Christmas day, then into Boxing Day, and finally on the morning of the twenty-seventh, we met our son, Spencer. We all fell in love with him, of course!

People often ask me how I found the courage to be a single parent with a five-week-old baby. For me, it wasn't about being brave; it was about surviving. I knew that something had to change, and it was up to me to make it happen. And I did.

My life is not perfect, but I am blessed to have created a family life for myself and my children together with Nick, my dad who now lives with us, Grace's dad, and our dog Holly. It's often messy and complicated. But it's also full of joy, laughter, and a lot of love. My children are loved by so many people, and that makes me happy.

Is this the family life I dreamed about as a child? No. It's totally different, but it works. This is real life, and it comes with the black, the white, and all the shades in between.

COMPILED by **KRISTY-LEA TRITZ**

Barb Heite

Barb Heite, with a master degree's in human dynamics, is the founder and transformational life coach of Amour de Soi, Love Your Soul, in Scottsdale, AZ. Barb is a published author of the book, *Beautiful Mess . . .A Journey to the Universe Within* —a compilation of writings expressing her feelings of discovering universal truths. Barb is passionate in her soul calling, purpose, teaching the practice of vulnerability; guiding private clients and groups onto the path of discovery of self-love, worth and acceptance. That happiness, love and trust is a choice and responsibility to consciously choose a blissful, joyful, fearless life.

www.barbheite.com
www.cuddlezone.net
www.soulsistersaz.com
www.completeholisticwellness.com
barbheite@gmail.com
www.facebook.com/pages/Barb-Heite/714270848662579
twitter.com/barbheite
youtube.com/barbheite
www.linkedin.com/pub/barb-heite/24/735/543

Chapter 6

THE POWER OF NO! BREAKING THE BONDS OF CO-DEPENDENCY

Barb Heite

At a young age, the cultivation of who I am and who I am supposed to be made me question myself. I lived in constant fear of upsetting people. My go-to behaviour was becoming invisible and doing what others wanted to survive my world. I ran within and got lost in my head and heart. I did not have control over much, but I had control of my thoughts.

Unfortunately, my thoughts were of the unloving nature. I never measured up. I was never good enough, smart enough, or pretty enough.

This constant judging and comparing myself with others skewed my reality of me. It was too painful to express my truths and be authentically me. I did not listen to my voice. I lived in an illusion of lies. I believed that others were somehow right about me, which meant I was wrong.

I chose to walk in the skewed convictions of others, letting my soul wash out into indistinctiveness. I no longer cared to reach out and connect. I was just living through the motions, unwilling to feel. When I questioned anything, I was told that I was imagining things, making up stories for attention, or that I was wrong when I said, "NO!"

I became confused. I no longer trusted myself. I believed

what was said to me—that I did not know what was best for me; that I must do A, B, C, and jump through hoops to be worthy and loved. The tasks for acceptance only became more exhaustive, and I just quit and became numb, no longer questioning choices made for me.

I was *just existing*.

I looked to others to validate every thought, interaction, and choice. I slipped seamlessly into co-dependency, starting with my family, friends, and then my spouse. I accepted, without question, the roles assigned to me from others. Willingly going along because it was the "right" thing to do. Clinging to the belief that if I could just make this person happy by giving what they required, I would be able to feel like I mattered, that I was cherished, wanted, and loved.

I was addicted to co-dependency. Like all addictions, there is always a price to pay. The price I paid was shattering. I had come to the place where the pain to hold in my "NO!" was too hard to ignore. My gradual descent into *just existing* was killing me—mentally, physically, and spiritually. This collapse in my world led to me questioning myself and who I was at the age of forty-six. And the first question I asked was, "What are you doing?"

What was I doing? Well, I was doing the best I could with what I knew, creating a beautiful mess called my life. I had gone through many therapy programs, workshops, schooling, and books. I could no longer disregard my life and just go along with being controlled and manipulated in the name of safety, justifying my actions with my skewed beliefs of what I defined as compassion, kindness, and love. I finally had to halt my world and stop, look, feel, and act.

I had to make a choice—to remain in fear or choose love and take responsibility for me. My codependent marriage was becoming chaotic and unbearable with each new awareness of who I was.

Then my life came to a standstill with the diagnosis of Stage 3 thyroid cancer. My world shifted in an instant. I had to decide, rather quickly, to trust what I knew to be true and take a leap of faith. I had to take a breath and trust someone else.

I found a life coach who based her coaching on the principles of real love. Her planting and watering of new seeds of who each of us are began to take root and grow within me. She instilled in me the lesson that we matter and are important; we each are loved beyond measure and are love and I believed her.

Let's face it, we all have been codependent at one time or another, starting from the first day we experience our physical world. As children, we are totally dependent on our caretakers. We would die without someone stepping in and meeting our most basic needs. As we grow and start experiencing our world and take chances, we start to display our independence.

At a young age, with the power of learning the word "NO!" we experience the rush of speaking up and screaming with enthusiasm "NO!" We discover the power of our voice and everything is answered with a "NO!" We are taught over and over that the world is not safe with "NO!" Then we mimic the expression of "NO!" and immediately are told not to say "NO!" We become confused and realize through being reprimanded that we have to obey and be good, which means not saying "NO!" So the message is internalized that speaking up is somehow wrong. And just as we are discovering who we are individually, the first seeds of doubt are planted and begin to take root and grow.

Over the years, the seed becomes grounded, entrenched into a perspective of self. The seed of self-doubt is watered by outside judgments, and we develop a high sensitivity to others who say "NO!" And we internalize and adjust our behaviour to be the good person in someone else's story of how the world ought to be.

We gradually, without conscious thought, operate from a place of fear. Wanting to be accepted, we start to perform, gathering bits and pieces of some type of validation. Through collecting praise for some accomplishment, seeking pleasure to hide in, going along with whatever to feel safe, or acting out and overpowering, we learn it feels good to perform (trade) for love and acceptance.

This information is internalized with our own belief system that forms judgments about ourselves or others. We create a verdict that is skewed in our interpretation of what is right or wrong in the world, making ourselves better than or less than another, continuing the cycle of trading. This gradual, seamless creation of our interpretations of the world feels real in the moment. We become seduced by the easiness of acquiring power, pleasure, praise, and safety to feel seen, accepted, and loved.

These behaviours, over time, are cultivated, and we will do whatever it takes to keep getting what we want. We are not able to identify what it is we lack—unconditional love and acceptance. Instead, we are confused that our "acts of kindnesses and love" requires more and more from us to maintain the feelings of acceptance and love. This feeling of having to *do more* begins to build into an internal struggle to scream out "NO!"

We stuff our "NOs" down and ignore our inner voice. We deny our natural curiosity for life and become angry and lash out. We are told we are wrong for pouring out our stuffed feelings. We become exceedingly diligent to others wants and needs. We conform, do as we are told, and go numb so we do not have to feel.

This cycle creates the one thing we are so afraid of: not being heard, seen, accepted, or loved. In our internal fighting with self, we get lost in the fear and forget to speak our own truths.

Instead, we show up wearing our masks of subtleties of behaviours. We control and manipulate our world to feel safe through lying, clinging, running, and attacking our self or others. We become a victim in our story, unconsciously choosing to believe that life is happening to us. We without question accept another perspective as our truth about who we are. We believe that someone else knows us better than ourselves.

Escaping life through some type of behaviour creates layers of interpretations that eventually will bloom into the reality of the person hiding in plain sight. We can become addicted to the behaviours of co-dependency and feel the need to perform in order to validate our own worth. This doesn't have to be the case.

Walking through the pain to unconditional love was the beginning of the end to my addiction to co-dependency.

With each truth shared, I began to experience the freedom of being responsible for how I show up in my world, understanding that I am always in choice to walk through hell or heaven.

It started with the simple step of choosing to see my life as a choice and to practice using my voice and saying "NO!" In doing so my urges to control and manipulate started to slip away. I started to shift from living in fear of doing something wrong to seeing life as an adventure, an exploration of possibilities and dreams. This practice of vulnerability, sharing my heart, created a world full of joy, happiness, kindness, compassion, tenderness and unconditional love.

I was finally free to create my own magic in my universe.

Dr. Biljana Karamehmedovic

Biljana Karamehmedovic, NaturOrthopathic Doctor, Ordained Holistic Health and Healing Minister, is a holistic personal transformation coach, author and speaker, as well as multiple foreign language interpreter and trainer.

As a passionate life LeapCoach, Biljana is making a difference in solopreneur's lives by helping them accomplish their miracles one Leap at the time. Her guidance and support is firmly based on universal metaphysical laws of personal and professional achievement. Through studying for almost three decades, human psychology and physiology, health, spirituality, human potential and success principles, as well as learning from top thought leaders and coaches in the field, Biljana's unique style offers her clients highly holistic approach to results they are seeking.

www.biljanakaramehmedovic.com
www.leapintoresults.com
support@leapintoresults.com

COMPILED by **KRISTY-LEA TRITZ**

Chapter 7

INVISIBLE POWER AND LEAPS OF FAITH: CULTIVATING INVISIBLE TO BRING OUT OBSERVABLE

Dr. Biljana Karamehmedovic

One of the greatest privileges I enjoy in this world is sharing my ability to fluently, immediately and precisely convey meaning from one language to another. Yet in that process, I have to remain as invisible as possible.

Allow me a few words of explanation. A language interpreter's job is to bridge the communication gap between people who don't speak the same language. It requires the interpreter to be (almost) invisible to allow for (almost) direct communication between those two parties.

Being the only one who completely understands all sides in this triad means that, as an interpreter, I have tremendous power and yet, for that power to properly work, it has to be correctly understood, employed, and nearly invisible.

Besides helping speakers involved to concentrate on each other, that invisibility allows me to detach, explore, and learn much more than I ever thought I could. It especially helps me realize that invisible power is the most important one to understand in both my interpreting and my coaching work.

Taking you on a quick journey back to the first years of my interpreting work—my family and I, in a tremendous leap of faith, came to the USA in 1995, not speaking a word of English. We had to rely on someone's interpretation for just about everything.

Not accepting it as permanent, I went on to rigorously study and learn the language of our new home. As I learned, I immediately started helping family, friends, and others in our growing refugee community.

Less than a year later, I had my first professional interpreting encounter and started the journey of cultivating empowered invisibility.

In the beginning, interpreting was extremely emotional, especially in healthcare settings. On top of all my personal pains, diagnoses, and health problems at that time—named as stress, anxiety, depression, numerous food and environmental allergies, skin and dental problems, gastritis, arthritis, etc.—every pain, every tragedy, every terminal diagnosis I interpreted was hurting me like it was mine and not the patient's.

And you bet it was exhausting and frustrating, to the point of inability to de-stress after my work was done, leaving me nauseous, sick, and wondering why none of the prescribed medications worked even though taken faithfully for so many years.

Continuing in the same direction was not possible anymore. It became unbearable and was not just affecting me but my family and friends as well. With all the other stress accumulated through experiencing war and settlement in a new country, getting drugged with more medications without any significant betterment ceased to be an option, especially when I realized my very young daughter was afraid of losing her mom forever.

Through all those times when my nerves were breaking down, and my world got dark and delusional, when my thoughts were racing at a speed faster than light, the Invisible tried to speak to me—in a language I did not understand at that time but one I finally knew I had to find an interpreter for.

I reached a breaking point and realized it was time to find out what was causing my suffering. Time to find out "why" as I broke the silence and spoke back to the Invisible loudly, for the first time in my life. As I was heard, the Invisible in me made me look for help in the opposite direction, in an unconventional way and on the inside instead of mainstream and from the outside.

As the saying goes: When the student is ready, the teacher shows up. So the answer to my desperate prayers came in the figure of a natural health practitioner, his listening, explanations of toxic, acidic body and his first recommendation—to begin my path toward healing with a fruit smoothie for breakfast.

Recognizing instantly the common sense in his words and remembering the great feeling from my younger years (when I was starting each and every day with a breakfast of fresh fruit picked from our family orchard), I quietly asked myself when did I actually switch from eating right to eating toxic? The answer "all these problems ago" was clear yet not important at the moment.

Important was that I found the answer making so much common sense that it was hard to contain my joy of finding it and the shock of realizing it was there all the time. It was

COMPILED by KRISTY-LEA TRITZ

knocking, asking, screaming, pinching, hurting... only this interpreter did not understand the language at that time. Thankfully there was one who did and the communication was, after many years, successfully re-established.

Ever since I clearly understood what a poisonous, acidic soup of food-like-products, coffee, nicotine, medications and especially stress and worry I was daily tasking my body with, it became clear what was in order. As for the first time seeing it possible, my goal became complete healing, which I named "Emo-Chemo-Financial Independence."

And my journey started with just that—seeing health possible and remembering that live fresh fruits will help to bring it back. The language of the body's inner invisible workings forever found the new interpreter, one determined to become fluent in it and help others understand it as well.

As life itself, our journeys are meant to evolve, so mine did too in all aspects. I went from English non-proficiency to national certification in healthcare interpreting; from abused, depressed, anxious, unhealthy introvert to confident, joyful, passionate spirit, healthcare interpreting trainer and life coach on principles of Natural Hygiene and Universal Laws.

Once broken, I today enjoy together with my family, a much higher level of health, joy and happiness (even though we are always work in progress). I am doing the work of my heart by helping others understand either the foreign language of another person, or the language of their inner Invisible, their souls and bodies trying to communicate deeper needs, higher desires, noble goals, life-grand purposes.

Through my trials and tribulation, success and

achievements, one underlying principle was making its way to my consciousness for a while. One that says: "Interpreting is everything."

When it first started forming in my consciousness, natural opposition to the thought was clearly defining it as a professional bias. As I was very heavily trained to not allow bias to affect meaning, I explored it further and found it to be true.

To interpret means to convey the meaning. It means to assign meaning. It means to define meaning. It means that every impulse, every signal, every data piece that reaches our brain through all senses and inner works, has to have meaning assigned. And who assigns the meaning? We do. Or we accept those given to us.

Each and every one of us is our own personal interpreter and meaning assigner. Some meanings we assign based on either our own or somebody else' rules and interpretation. Most of them we absorbed from our immediate surroundings very early in life—from parents, family and friends, media, society's institutions... They all become part of our Invisible way before we are mature enough to decide if we want them or not, if they serve us well or not. Those meanings formed our deepest unquestioned beliefs and those are driving our decisions, our actions and behaviour, and of course our results.

You can't see those beliefs directly as they are part of your Invisible. But you can hear, feel, and see very well their consequences and results in many different ways through the different languages they speak: languages called low self-confidence, guilt, shame, pain, depression, anxiety, obesity, divorce, addictions, diseases, bankruptcies... you get the idea.

Listen to your own language, your self-talk, feel the languages of your body, see the results in your life and break the silence. Speak up, speak back directly to your Invisible and ask for the real meaning, real message. Or find an appropriate interpreter practitioner to help you.

Silence is golden only when you listen with attention and intention. So listen; listen deeply; listen actively. Your Invisible is trying to get you to learn the truth, what it truly means. The way you interpret (or assign meaning of) anything and everything in your life defines your decisions, actions and of course results. Interpreting is everything. Always ask what it means.

Often, it means it's time to drop the past, to grow in present, assign fresh meanings, dust off those timeless ones and once again claim your true Invisible Power of Light, Love and Abundance. For that is your Birthright, your Spirit, your True Nature.

And often it also means it is time to dare to leap. Leaps are where magic happens. And without the leap, faith stays alone, interpreting goes unheard, Invisible gets dark, painful and scary.

Take the leap of faith. Cultivate your Invisible so it can speak and shine in its glory now and always and bring out observable. Your life wants to be lived and lived abundantly.

Will you let it?

Charlene Schmidt

Charlene Schmidt is a health and wellness warrior. She believes everyone should have the choice to live healthy lives. When she is not helping others live healthier lives, she can be found volunteering her time with her church and community. Charlene is a woman whom her friends call powerful in her purpose.

www.esanteorganics.com/hopeforyourhealth
char.schm@hotmail.com
facebook.com/hopeforyourhealth

COMPILED by **KRISTY-LEA TRITZ**

Chapter 8

I WAS HEALED! MIGRAINES, MY CHILDHOOD ROBBER

Charlene Schmidt

Just five years old, I sat there, feeling what was happening. I knew it was coming on again.

Migraines were taking over my childhood. I didn't understand what was happening to me. I was young and scared. As the migraine intensified, my vision was lost and replaced by auras. Parts of my vision were missing.

As I sat in the dark room, I couldn't even lie down. I was just trying to be as still as possible. I felt alone and isolated. I wasn't in control of what was happening and it brought me such fear.

Sitting there in the darkness, the migraine's effects took over and parts of my body became numb. Starting in my left hand, a three-inch-wide path would travel all the way up my arm, into my shoulder. Stopping in my shoulder, the numbness would then travel to my left foot, move up through the left side of my leg, back up into my left shoulder, and into my chest.

Feeling the numbness in my chest, where my heart was,

made me feel like I was having a heart attack, which made it difficult for me to breathe. Feeling sick to my stomach, I knew this experience was going to last me hours and then would leave me alone!

Migraines were robbing me of my childhood. I wasn't able to play as carefree as other children. I knew it would only be a matter of time before another one would strike and the whole cycle would begin again. It made me feel helpless because there was nothing I could do. No matter how much I wished I didn't have them, they would always come back.

I could always tell when one would be coming on due to my loss in vision. My mom tried to help by taking me to all kinds of doctors who did tons of tests, trying to figure out what was going on. No one seemed to have the answer in how to stop them or at least provide me with relief so I could have my childhood. I had to accept that it was a hereditary thing; my grandmother also suffered from migraines. My childhood was just going to be different. It would be filled with the dark and pain.

Troubles with my neck were prevalent as well. Even at a young age, I went to chiropractors and sought treatment to help find relief. I just wanted to find solace and a place of peace rather than being scared.

As I got older, I had to be careful when I was out. Something as simple as a flash from the sunlight off a car bumper would instantly trigger a migraine. Ceiling fans were another trigger—the fans passed through the light and made it flash. Flickering candles were also a trigger. I would blow candles out no matter where I was.

I always had to be on the alert for triggers to try and ensure that I didn't have to suffer a migraine. It was my way of controlling the environment around me because of the fear of knowing what I experience with migraines. I wanted to avoid them at all costs.

In my latter teens, I became addicted to 222s. They helped me function in public spaces. I wanted to have fun with my friends and go out places. Taking 222s allowed me to partake in the bar scene and concerts—without them I wouldn't be able to function. Anytime I felt a migraine coming on, I would take them. Honestly, a lot of times I would take them to prevent migraines from happening. I would just pop a few 222s and was good to go. Here I was, addicted and drinking alcohol while taking them.

Later in life, I got married when my son was just a year old. I was in such pain with neck issues and migraines that I found it difficult to function at any level. The pain had taken over my life.

I was also attending church and had become a born-again Christian. It was shortly after that I began that journey in my life where I experienced the most intense pain.

I was in such pain I had to lie down on my couch. I didn't want to move, the pain was so intense. It was shooting through me. Lying on my stomach with my son still in bed, I thought, "How am I going to take care of my son? I can't even move! I am just in so much pain."

As I lay there, I began to pray for my neck. I prayed that the pain would end, that my neck would get better, and that I would be able to take care of my son as a mother is supposed to. I just didn't know what to do anymore.

The pain was so intense, I didn't even have the strength really to pray. Praying was all I could do in that moment though, as the pain slowly took over every inch of my thoughts.

A vision began to take place as I lay there in agony. It was the strangest feeling. I began to feel like I was rocking back and forth. I could see myself lying at the bottom of a boat as the boat rocked. I was lying at the bottom of the boat just the same way I was lying on my couch—n my stomach with my face planted in the cushion. Just rocking and rocking. I was laying there thinking, what am I doing lying in the bottom of this boat?

As I was thinking this, an old lady came up to me. She laid her hands on me and began praying over me. Right at that precise moment, I saw a big beam of light come out of my ceiling with a boom that was audible. It hit me in the back of my neck and in between my shoulder blades. Instantly, heat crossed my shoulder blades and went up and down my spine.

It was an instant healing. I knew I was healed. I got up

and I could move. I knew that I had just been a witness to a miracle in my own life.

Anytime God brings healing to your life, in whatever form that is, the devil will try and create doubt in you. I questioned whether that had really happened to me. Had I really experienced healing of my migraines?

Even though I was healed and my migraine went away, I would still experience symptoms. I knew they were not actual symptoms. I knew this was a test for me. I had to accept that I had been healed and could go off my medication. Withdrawal happened from my 222s, but it was nothing like it could have been. I was living almost in a state of shock. It was, at first, difficult to believe that I had been healed from the most dreadful thing in my life—my childhood robber.

Miracles do still happen and having gone through my own, it has taught me a few things I feel are important to share. My healing taught me never to give up. I wanted to give up. In the moment of my healing, I was at a place where I just didn't know if I could live with the pain anymore. It taught me to pray for what it is I want to be healed from. Being healed also taught me to appreciate things in life more than I had.

I heard of miracles happening, but when I experienced my own, it began a journey that profoundly changed my life.

Miracles happen in our everyday lives. We are often just

too busy to see them. As humans, we let everything around us consume us, whether it's pain—like I had experienced—or work. It is important you take time to notice the little miracles around you: flowers blooming, children being born, pain being healed, families taking time to care for each other. Appreciate each and every moment you are given, for in each moment lies a miracle.

I am still today migraine-free!

Christine Merritt

Christine Merritt is a board certified integrative nutrition coach and wellness advocate with doTERRA International. She is dedicated to empowering women to heal their digestion and their spirit and create a life of financial freedom and time freedom. She teaches her team to empower other women to grow personally while learning how to manifest a rich and abundant life. Christine is a wife and mother living in Austin, Texas. She is an author, speaker, blogger, and educator. She loves to travel, read, shop, and get pampered. She is avidly interested in spiritual growth and studies the law of attraction.

www.christinemerritt.com
christine@christinemerritt.com
facebook.com/innerharmonyforlife
twitter.com/inrharmony4life
linkedin.com/in/innerharmonyforlife

COMPILED by **KRISTY-LEA TRITZ**

Chapter 9

SOBRIETY MY ROCK: HEALING ALCOHOLISM AND MANIFESTING FREEDOM WITH SELF-LOVE

Christine Merritt

I spent my entire adult life in a cage, ruled by alcohol. I called it "having fun," "partying," and "just relaxing," but the sad reality was that it was none of those things. It was a way to hide from feelings I didn't want to feel. It was a way to not live my life to its true potential. It was a way of hiding my precious self deep inside, and it kept me from discovering the talents and loving heart I had to share with the world.

For thirty years, up to April 2013, my day-to-day life consisted of thinking only about my next drink. Even though I didn't drink all day long—mainly just in the evenings—I was still THINKING about drinking in the moments that I was not drinking. It consumed my thoughts and created a reality of hell. Not having a glass of wine in my hand made me feel uncomfortable.

When I couldn't hide behind the high of alcohol, I wanted to hide from the world. I didn't want to face the person in the mirror because I didn't like her very much. I saw myself as weak and pathetic because I couldn't be perfect, and I felt like I couldn't make people love me for me. I had external conditions I felt made me unlovable. And I had to control every situation.

When I figured out I couldn't be perfect and in control at

all times, it was just easier to drink, to forget and go the opposite direction to "I don't give a shit" island. My boat sailed there daily and I hung out there, not caring, not loving myself.

My relationships were all based on "who would be fun to party with" or "who could take care of me" because I was incapable of caring for myself. I sought love from men who were just as insecure as myself and wondered why my relationships always tanked. I could see I was hurting myself by making the same mistakes over and over, but I just kept chugging along, fuelled by alcohol and the belief that wine would make it all OK.

I dealt with stress by drinking, and in 2011 and 2012 I had the most stressful years of my life. In 2011, I worked at the worst job in history and had constant stress from my father-in-law's cancer. In 2012, I had two foot surgeries, lost my father-in-law to cancer, and went through a four-month home remodel from hell while battling an extreme stomach flu.

The drinking escalated, and finally on New Year's Eve, as I was ringing in 2013, I knew I had to get sober. I made a resolution to drink less wine and eat more veggies. Well, we all know what happens with resolutions—and guess what? Mine was no different.

It wasn't long before I was drinking "just on the weekends." That turned into Fridays too. I had started nutrition school, and I was feeling bad every day. I knew from what I was learning in school that what I was doing to my body was slowly killing me.

If I didn't get help, I would eventually be bloated,

chronically ill, and in pain. I had already been experiencing pains in my joints and having major stomach and digestion issues, plus insomnia. On top of the physical symptoms of alcohol dependency, I was feeling massive guilt around what I was doing to myself and my family. I was a complete mess.

I went to the doctor and the best thing happened. Most people wouldn't think this is a good thing but I was diagnosed with systemic Candida (yeast) overgrowth. It was good because I was told I had to be on a special diet and take medication for six weeks... and I was told not to drink alcohol.

Well, "No problem," I thought. I had quit before, during both of my pregnancies, so I took my last drink on April 19, 2013.

The first weeks were tough. I was dealing with the yeast die-off and was so sick. But then something happened. I looked back to the past and realized I was a complete mess and I was unhappy being a slave to alcohol addiction.

I started reading *A Return to Love* by Marianne Williamson. I had a sudden epiphany. I realized I am a child of God. I am pure light and love. Nothing outside of me defines me. Not the stress, the parties, relationships, the money, the jobs, things I own—none of it, not even the alcohol. I am me and I am love, just as I am.

I am also human and I make mistakes, and I realized I had to forgive myself. I had to forgive the other humans who hurt me because they are created out of pure love too. I also realized that if I wasn't sober, I couldn't have the life I was creating for myself. Alcohol and its side effects did not fit with my vision of my future.

Because I am a powerful loving human being, I can CREATE my life to be the way I want it to be. I can manifest a life of love, happiness, and freedom. I can deal with problems and stress in a healthy way. I can honour the body I was given by God and be my true authentic self.

Thoughts are powerful. As I would stand in the shower, with my new sober mindset, I would imagine I was on a rock—my rock of sobriety. The water cascading down was washing away all of the negative thoughts. I have never felt more love in my life than I did at that moment. It was love FOR MYSELF and my Creator—pure LOVE. That is truly the way out of any prison: choosing love over fear... because fear is the prison.

My favourite quote by Marianne Williamson sums up fear quite nicely: "Our deepest fear is not that we are inadequate. Our deepest fear is that we are powerful beyond measure. It is our Light, not our darkness, that most frightens us."

For years I was scared, and I thought it was the fear of not being perfect or not having control, but what I was really scared of was my power, my light, the goodness inside that I didn't want to let out because I felt I didn't deserve to be loved for myself. I was damaged and wanted to hide. Now that I finally see the truth of my true beauty, I can no longer hide it.

I spent hours walking in nature just marvelling at the massive love emanating from the plants and trees. Every living thing on the earth gives me love. I take it in, and it gives the strength I need to get through the day. I honoured my body by eating whole, real food, juicing, and doing other self-care practices—such as dry brushing, meditation, and self-hypnosis. I focused on growing new, healthy, loving friendships and found a tribe of like-minded people to connect with. I truly believe that making the decision to enroll in holistic nutrition school saved my life.

My intuition has also gotten stronger. By healing my gut from the damage caused by years of alcohol abuse, I made myself much more in tune with my inner voice. My soul was calling out to me, and I intuitively knew I needed to remove all medication and chemicals from my body. I have been using therapeutic essential oils as natural medicine and giving my body the chance to heal. My body is thanking me by feeling better and better every day, and my spirit is healing as well.

I keep the sober mindset by remembering the hell I went through but also by cherishing my strength and thanking God for bringing me to this point. My story has meaning, and now I know why I am here on the earth. I was sent here to help others find their peace on earth. If I only help one person by getting my story out, then my job is done.

Every moment in my new life is magical. I feel so free to give my whole heart to those who need me—most importantly, myself. If you think that the statement "you cannot fully love others until you love yourself" is just a cliché, I'm here to tell you it is anything but. Realizing you are a valuable, loving being and actually LIVING that way in every moment allows you to be present to your loved ones and appreciate every single moment.

My sobriety is my rock. It gives me the chance to be the best me possible, and I have God in my grasp. I love my life now, beyond words, and I am using my newfound power to lift up other women and give them the opportunity to see themselves in a new light. Peace is an amazing thing. It can free you from thoughts of self-hatred, lack, and negativity.

As long as I know I am standing on my rock and I can hug myself and really love my true self, I am free.

Cindy Leavitt

Cindy Leavitt is passionate about her walk with the Lord Jesus Christ! Both Proverbs 31 and Mike, her husband of 33 years, gave her permission to overcome fear and become a real estate investor. Now she helps educate others to do the same! Her philosophy is more about increasing cash flow than merely owning cute little buildings (though some are indeed cute)! She and her husband raised and home schooled five children, two of whom purchased their first investment property by the age of 18. She is a woman filled with joy and laughter. Glorifying God with her passions and talents is her greatest mission, along with encouraging others to do the same.

www.kingdomcashflow.net
facebook.com/cindyleavitt
twitter.com/cindyleavitt
linkedin.com/in/CDLeavitt
cindy@kingdoncashflow.net

COMPILED by **KRISTY-LEA TRITZ**

Chapter 10

I CHOOSE TO WORSHIP: HOW TO WALK IN THE JOY OF THE LORD AFTER THE DEATH OF A CHILD

Cindy Leavitt

King David was a worshiper. He is my favorite worshiper. He and I have been buds for years. I have learned to cry out to a merciful God by using his example, praise by his example and to worship through hardship by his example. Deeper intimacy with the Father always follows. I have learned vulnerability and transparency by his example. Deeper intimacy has always followed. I GET David. We are tight!

In 2 Samuel:12, David's son was dying. He fasted. He prayed. He contended for healing for his son. He was a mess. He wouldn't eat or allow others to pick him up off of the floor. His son died. When he found out, he got up off of the floor, washed his face, put on some clean clothes, and went to worship.

I have meditated on that Scripture many times over the years. I got a glimpse of a deeper worship experience by David's response after his son died. I *sooo* get David! Today, I understand him even more.

My daughter had cancer. I cried out to God to heal her. I fasted and prayed. There were times that others could not pick me up off of the floor. The last time was just days ago, the day our daughter died. I laid across the body that she left and wailed in agonizing grief.

COMPILED by **KRISTY-LEA TRITZ**

It's possible I'm not as courageous as David but I don't really think it's up for comparison. I am still a worshiper. I will worship through this hardship and deeper intimacy will come.

In the infancy of this habit, it was a faith-filled discipline. Now I am simply motivated by what is to come, just knowing that He is worthy. I fully expect deeper intimacy to follow. I have no question.

Not one inkling of God's sovereignty shifted when David's son died, nor when my daughter died. God's worthiness to be worshiped did not change one iota. He is worthy of worship, worthy of praise, and worthy of adoration. David had experienced God's sovereignty, His mercy, His deliverance, His love, and His friendship on so many other occasions that he didn't have to stop and ask himself if he should go worship. He just went and worshiped. That is where I am at. David had his reasons. I have mine.

Here's a snapshot of the worshiper that I am: I can't hold a tune, I don't remember words to songs...EVER. When I dance I break things because grace is not a part of any movement that I make— except on the tennis or volleyball court... on a good day.

Just over a decade ago, I was driving down the road, bellowing the lyrics to a worship song at the top of my lungs. As usual, I got the words and syllables mixed up, and what came out of my mouth proclaimed I was awesome and worthy of praise. When I realized what I said, I was horrified and quickly clasped one hand over my mouth.

I was in mid-repentance mode when, in my spirit, I heard

the Father let out the biggest belly laugh. I saw Him throw his head back and grab His belly while it shook with laughter. After hearing several seconds of laughter, He said, "You make me laugh! I love how quirky you are."

I burst into tears and had to pull the car over. The thought of provoking my Heavenly Father, the God of the universe, to a deep belly laugh moved me more than I can say. The thought of Him enjoying me changed me....FOREVER! The thought that I could surprise Him with my child-like goofiness changed me FOREVER.

Every interaction that I have with Him changes me FOREVER. I was so deeply touched to get a glimpse of the Father's heart toward me... toward us. He adores us! It is much too easy to think that He is a harsh, mean, punishing God than it is to accept His unconditional love and be transformed by it.

There I was mid-repentance, and He was simply delighted in who I am, including my clumsiness. He was celebrating and so very happy with my awkward, unprofessional, un-Hillsong attempt at adoring Him. That would be similar to me leaning over to kiss my husband, tripping mid-kiss, and bashing our faces together. (Don't laugh—that happens to everyone... right?)

It seemed as though I ruined a beautiful, intimate moment, but it only increased when I was just me, in all of my blundering glory. I was forever changed because He loves me enough to show me and tell me, right in the middle of me being me—so very clumsy and unpracticed and raw in my moments of adoring Him.

Worship only increased! Adoration erupted from me, and

I was immersed in His presence. We think He wants perfection when He just wants us, just as we are, to approach a throne room so filled with grace that all desire for anything else disappears, all depravity disintegrates. We think that we have to work and work and work to worship, to get rid of our sin before approaching Him, but He already did that. It is finished. It truly is finished!

I could share dozens upon dozens of similar experiences I have had with my Abba, but I have two other points to share.

We have prayed for every one of our children and grandchildren to develop and grow in their relationship with Jesus Christ. We aren't ones to pray for them to just step inside the gate for safekeeping. We don't pray for their butts to be greased so when the door slams shut, they will slide right in. We pray for Davidic hearts. We pray for passionate hearts running hard after Him, slaying giants along the way.

More often than not I feel inadequate in my prayer life, but the God I serve is so very generous. I am learning it is much more about His generosity than my works. I have been giddy with joy that this prayer has been generously answered. Katelyn lived passionately for our Lord. She lived loving others and sharing what she knew of Him. His generosity draws me to deeper intimacy with Him.

Secondly, I have prayed that my children would experience a greater intimacy with the Father than I have ever known. I am saturated with a childish joy that my daughter is witnessing so much more. My heart is full and overflowing. I don't know what heaven will be like, other than gold so pure that it is clear—and other descriptions given in Scripture.

I have to say, as a woman who doesn't place much value in jewelry, gems, or precious metals, that the whole gold thing just doesn't speak to me. I don't think that's what I'll have my eyes on. I will have my eyes set as flint on the most beautiful thing I have ever witnessed—the eyes of the One Who loves me because I am quirky, the One Whom I make laugh, the One Whom I sing incomplete and politically and spiritually incorrect songs to, and He just soaks them in because He loves my adoring voice! He loves me! I make Him belly laugh! If you ever heard me sing, you would gain a whole new understanding of His unconditional love.

Katelyn is no longer gasping for air but she is breathing in the presence and aroma of the One Who adores her. There is no greater joy. She transitioned from misery to glory, but this is less about the lack of suffering and much, much more about being in the presence of the King of Kings, He Who is pure joy.

One of my greatest prayers has been answered: that my child may experience the presence of my loving God even more than I. I am overwhelmed with His goodness.

Just after Katelyn released her last breath, we could see glory on her face. That is the only way to describe what I saw. I actually looked up at the ceiling to see if someone had turned a spotlight on her face. There was no spotlight. I have witnessed a new definition of peace. It was written on her face that day. She had to have been looking into His eyes. I cannot contain the joy that bubbles out of me since that day. She was beautiful. It was beautiful.

I have laughed more than I have cried since Katelyn died.

That is going to make some people uncomfortable. I am okay with that. Sometimes discomfort is just what we need.

He is worthy to be praised in every manner possible. I have yet to dance naked on my rooftop. Watch out neighbours!

Debbie Franklin

Debbie Franklin is a successful entrepreneur, wife, and mother. She is a city girl who lives on a small farm with her country boy husband and their English Cream Golden Retrievers, cat, horses, and cattle. She has a passion for helping business moms create more time and focus and get the support in their business, schedule, and life to allow them more freedom to do the things they love! Developing a business that you not only love but also supports you can provide a harmonious home for your family. Debbie understands the role of being a mom (and a businesswoman) and that you are the "heart of your family."

www.debbiefranklin.com
contact@debbiefranklin.com
facebook.com/ithedebbiefranklin
twitter.com/debbiefranklin
www.linkedin.com/in/debbiefranklin55

Chapter 11

CREATE A NEW FAMILY LEGACY! HEALING MY PAST TO LIVE A BETTER FUTURE

Debbie Franklin

Still unsure why I was the one who needed help, I sat in the counsellor's office waiting for my name to be called. I was nervous and felt vulnerable and exposed. What did he see that I didn't?

We'd been having some behavioural issues with our oldest son and had sought out counselling to "fix him." The counsellor talked to my husband and myself to see what was happening in our home and if there were any marital problems that could be contributing to the situation. The next appointment, he spoke to our son privately and then asked to talk with me.

I sat on the couch and listened to the counsellor explain to me that I was the one he needed to work with in solving the problems we were having with our son. I needed to learn how to respond to situations rather than reacting to them. Helping my son depended upon me changing.

I left the counsellor's office feeling like a horrible mom—it was my fault my son was struggling. I thought I was a good mom—it was all I ever wanted to be. How could I be failing at something I loved so much?

I knew at that moment I had two choices: Walk away and things stay status quo, or come back to the counsellor and do the work he was asking me to do. I chose the latter.

The receptionist called my name to go back into the counsellor's office. I sat down, and after a few pleasantries, he began to ask me about my childhood—not my most favourite topic. When did my parents get divorced, when did they remarry, what were their new spouses like, etc.?

My parents divorced when I was about two and a half years old. My dad stayed in southern California, and my mom moved to northern California. I don't remember much of this time of my childhood. My most vivid memories begin when I was around five, a few years after my mom remarried.

My stepdad had a drinking problem, a bad temper, and a very sick sense of humour. My mom was unhappy, and the older I got the more I struggled between wanting to leave and stop living with my mom and going to live with my dad. My dad had also remarried, and while my stepmom was a good person, she wasn't good with handling children. I felt like I didn't belong or wasn't wanted in either place.

My mom eventually divorced my stepdad, but within a short period of time remarried again. While this man didn't drink and was good to my mom, he was domineering, and to my horror I found he liked to watch me undress when she wasn't home.

The counsellor asked if I ever told anyone about what was happening in our home. No, I never did. I pondered that for a long time. Why didn't my brothers and I ever say anything? Why didn't I tell my dad what was happening with either of my stepdads? Why didn't I tell my mom that I caught her second husband watching me? The counsellor explained that my need to be with my mom was greater than my fear of not being with her. I knew by telling that I would be taken away from her.

The counsellor then asked me about my first marriage. I had married a year after I graduated high school to a man I had been dating since I was sixteen. He drank and had a bad temper. As I walked down the aisle, I kept asking myself what I was doing. I didn't want to marry him, but I did it anyway. I was scared not to. We divorced a few years later, and I was blessed to find a wonderful man to share my life and have children with.

Looking at my childhood, myself, and who I was at that moment wasn't easy. I didn't like what I saw. Just as we bring baggage from a previous marriage into a new one, I soon realized how much we do the same from our childhood into our parenting.

I had always been told I had a bad temper. I didn't have a bad temper. I was an angry child trapped in an adult body. The more I learned about myself, the more I wanted to know and understand how I had become who I was. It was as an observer, not as a judge.

My mom and I had long conversations about her first marriage to my dad and why she left him, as well as why she married my first stepdad. What I learned is that my grandfather was abusive and an alcoholic. My mom married what she knew. My dad was a hard worker and a kind, loving man. My mom didn't understand that kind of love. She had only experienced her parent's marriage, which was a jealous, angry, and possessive kind of love.

The biggest awareness for me was when I realized we are

a collection of not only our childhood experiences but our parents' as well. We have to understand the patterns of our generations to move forward. I love Maya Angelou's quote: "Do the best you can until you know better. Then when you know better, do better."

The counsellor was asking me to know better, so I could do better. It wasn't about blame or judgment. He knew I was doing the best I could with what I had been taught. Now, it was my job to do better.

The hardest part of changing was being vigilant of using my new awareness for responding to situations instead reacting. Instead of letting things build up, I had to deal with each issue at that moment—not wait until I had no patience left. This meant I had to speak up and voice what was bothering me, what wasn't working, what I needed, and do it in a way that I felt heard.

When things got out of control, I had to stop and take a breath and remove myself from the situation until I could calmly handle it.

Things do sometimes get worse before they get better. My children didn't understand the new way of doing things, especially my oldest son. He and I were used to yelling and not listening to each other. It was my job to show him a different way, and that job sometimes was more than I was equipped for. It took practice and consistency.

I wished I had known who I was before I became a parent. I wish I understood what things unconsciously triggered anger responses from me that had nothing to do with the situation. I could have released my need to control everything around me if I had known it was about my need to feel safe and nothing about needing to control others. Life would have been less stressful if I could have relaxed and trusted the future instead of my need to anticipate what was going to happen in every situation from years of living with alcoholics and trying to eliminate possible things that could make them angry.

Learning about myself gave me freedom from the past and the ability to trust and enjoy the future. Exploring my past, my parents and grandparents, and my choices wasn't about criticizing and judging, it is was about observing and understanding in order to learn and do better. It is something to be done with love and compassion for oneself. It isn't an opportunity to judge or blame others for their choices and decisions, but to open the door for understanding and forgiveness.

Discovering my best qualities, strengths, and weaknesses allowed me to be authentic and become a positive role model for my children. I learned to trust myself and have confidence in who I am, which gave me the ability to allow my children to be who they are, the freedom to discover their own inner strengths and weaknesses so they can make the best decisions they can for their lives.

As a mom, we can help our children grow to their fullest potential. Once we understand that we bring our baggage into our parenting style, as well as into the relationship with our children, we can change how we react and respond to them—from who we truly are, not from who we were conditioned to be.

I am so thankful and blessed to have done the hard work. My three beautiful children are now all grown with families of their own, and we have the best relationship. I looked at my past to understand where I have come, but I have left it behind in order to be who I am.

My intention in sharing my story is to inspire and motivate moms to leave behind their past and create a new legacy by connecting to their true self, embracing their uniqueness, and discovering the true spirit of who they are —allowing them to enjoy life and the journey of motherhood; changing the lives of their husband, children, and those around them.

Eleni Szemeti

Serial seven-figure entrepreneur and mum of three, Eleni Szemeti has scoured the planet (literally) to discover cutting-edge techniques, shortcuts, and surefire formulas for success.

She has studied the psychological, social, and heart of what it takes to really unlock success.

You'll know you are in safe hands and will get the quickest route to success when you are being guided by someone who can manage to grow herself and do the heavy lifting of multiple seven- figure businesses at the same time as raising three beautiful and treasured kids.

www.bouncehub.com.au
eleni@bouncehub.com.au
facebook.com/eleni.szemeti
twitter.com/bouncehub
au.linkedin.com/in/eleniszemeti

COMPILED by **KRISTY-LEA TRITZ**

Chapter 12

THE ROSEBUD, THE GIFT AND THE MIRACLE: FROM ADVERSITY TO JOY IN THE QUEST TO MOTHERHOOD

Eleni Szemeti

We have all heard the saying that "we often teach what we need to learn." Little did I know how literal this was. I am still learning lessons that guide me and serve others. Did I know what my higher purpose would be at the school where I was teaching science and math? I learned lessons in faith, community, and family. I learned to be inspired and to be inspirational. I learned there was hope when there seemed to be none. Most of all, I learned the power of love and resilience.

As a child, I was bullied and harassed and teased for being a child of migrant parents. I knew no different, and it was my first tough lesson. My whole life has been a long journey as I learned to look after others and be a protector and champion for the underdog. I wish someone had taught me to also care for *me*.

I placed so much value in the word *family* that I sometimes lost myself. Today, I know that family can mean so many different things to so many people. I hope my journey in creating my family can give you some hope, some inspiration, and help you find your peace in the world.

Family: it gives us our sense of identity, teaches us values, and sets up our beliefs about ourselves and the world around us. For some, it is the best lesson they will ever have. For others, it's their nightmare. The teenagers I came across, the stories that sometimes were too horrific to imagine, kept me going. There was always hope—if people were just willing to be there, so much healing could be achieved. When you come from a place of love, you can inspire others. You can heal the world.

One of my strongest values is one of family, community, and belonging. My journey to create the family I wanted was not an easy road. I always wanted to have a big family. I just wanted my kids to feel the power of a family when I wasn't around—something I did not have growing up and desperately wanted. I went a long way to achieve my dream. I overcame many hurdles and battles within myself but never gave up.

The biggest lesson of all for me was one that I never expected or wanted. By the age of thirty-one, I had miscarried seven times. I was told by some not-so-friendly, unoptimistic doctors to move on with my life. *Give up... you will never be a mother. Live your life and make something of yourself, as motherhood is not going to be in your future.*

I researched and read and scrutinized medical journals for answers. Early during my eighth pregnancy, I went to my gynaecologist with some research I had uncovered. Not wanting to believe what I had found but equally not wanting to dismiss my hopes, she helped me. I took the hormones and prayed.

Alas, at ten weeks, just like all the others, I started bleeding. My heart sank as I waited for the ultrasound. Once again, I braced myself to look at a screen with no life, no hope—my dreams gone.

The very kind and patient doctor placed the warmed scanner on my belly, and I closed my eyes as I did not want to face another loss. I once again felt like my chance at motherhood was being ripped from me.

The Rose Bud

Gently, I was asked to open my eyes. What was this? A small round bud with little arms and legs waving around. This was it! A sight I had never seen before. A baby that was well and truly alive.

I spent the next few months in disbelief. At eight months along, I woke up with an uneasy feeling. I stayed at home because I felt something was wrong. By 5 pm, I had my first contraction. I could barely believe what was to happen next.

When all hope is gone, what do you do? Sometimes, I overthink and overanalyze, and that can make you afraid to take chances. It leads you to procrastination. It stops you from moving forward into the next step of your awesome life.

What's Holding You Back?

Is it your why? Your fear? The voice in your head telling you no? We can listen to the voice in our head and fail to move forward. Or we can take a chance, fall, stand up, and learn the lesson we were supposed to learn all along. That was the lesson I had to learn with my ninth pregnancy.

Things could not have been going any better. I was at week sixteen and just received results from some routine tests. Not ones with results I wanted to read: your baby has a

1 in 9 chance of having spina bifida.

Further tests didn't look promising. Sitting in surgery, I was appalled at what I heard next: *No one should knowingly bring a disabled child into the world. I think it's best to abort.* I sit here today and wonder how many other couples are told the same thing.

I chose to continue the pregnancy. I had waited a long time to become a mother, and if God wanted me to have this child, then there was a reason and I was willing to find out what it was.

The Gift

I felt a little lost with not knowing what to expect, but the choice would be taken from me just five weeks later. I felt a gush of warmth, and when I stood up, there was blood everywhere. I was rushed to the hospital and told to prepare myself because I was in early labor—with zero chance of survival for the baby.

I was given lifesaving blood and then waited. Weeks went by, then a few more weeks. Then a few more. Everyone had been wrong. This baby wanted to be here and was showing such a fighting spirit.

The Miracle

At forty, my yearning to complete my family was surging through my whole being. I decided to participate in an overseas trial for older women. I traveled to Canada and embarked on my final quest. It was a difficult journey. My father was ill, and I was so far away from him. It broke my heart but his encouragement was something I always treasured. He was the one supporter in my life that I could count on. I told him of my plans, and he gave me his blessing.

My first attempt at IVF failed, and I was told, due to my age, they were only willing to attempt once more. Then it would be over for me.

I was back in Australia when I got the call that everything was lined up. However, I needed to get over there in the following month. I spoke to my dad, who by this time was in the hospital. He was excited and gave me his blessing. He couldn't wait to meet his grandchild.

On May 23, 2006, my baby entered the world. He had dark curly hair just like my dad, and I swore I saw him there with me, smiling at us. He had passed over a few months before, never having the chance to meet his grandson. Every day he is with us, though. His spirit and guidance are always present. My baby was the final gift to complete my family.

The Miracle really was the missing part to our family. We had longed for him, and he filled a gap in our hearts.

Let me take you back a bit.

What happened to the Rose Bud? As I mentioned, this little baby was a bud on the screen at just ten weeks. At eight months, she entered the world. I knew there was a reason to stay home that day. She healed my heart after so many losses.

The Gift didn't want to give up. After nine long months, he entered the world. Always a drama, he managed to get the cord wrapped around his neck and arm. However, he was my little fighter. He joined our family and is healthy and truly an inspiration to us all.

Today, I have three beautiful, healthy children. I have been a host mother to four teenagers and am blessed to have never given up!

Today, my family is complete. I am grateful for the lessons I have learned throughout all the trials. I learned strength, endurance, belief and faith. To trust myself and to take risks when I believed them to be true and right. I learned to never give up, no matter the trials and pitfalls before me, no matter how painful it was, how it wrenched at my heart all those times. I learned that I had the love and support of MY family around me when it counted the most.

When you want something more than you want to breathe, you know you have found your passion. You have found your dream, you have found your WHY. I found mine, and I pray that you, too, find yours.

Sometimes, the WHY in your head reflects your fears. It can be the voice telling you NO, holding you back from the next big step in your life. You can listen to this voice in your head and fail to move forward. Or, you can take a chance, fall, stand up and go again, and learn the lesson which life was trying to teach you all along. This is what I did. I discovered my WHY, the desire to have family, and every time I fell down, I got back up again, more determined to make it happen.

So, let me ask you—what is your why?

Janiece Montano

Janiece Montano is an emergency medical technician by trade. She was born in Durango, Colorado, and raised in Aztec, New Mexico. She became a district manager for a skincare health and wellness company, Bioceutica LLC, in Mesa, Arizona. She is a loving, giving, caring person, and her passion is to help others. Her latest project is a nonprofit organization that provides support for military families. When she isn't working her business, she spends time hanging out with her kids, gardening, and cooking—and she even brews her own beer.

www.bioceutica.com/janiece
janiece_consulting@yahoo.com
facebook.com/pages/AWSM-Arizona-Women-Support- Movement/1510337932534706

COMPILED by **KRISTY-LEA TRITZ**

Chapter 13

White Picket fence: life after divorce

Janiece Montano

My childhood dream was to meet the man of my dreams, get married, have children, and live happily ever after in a house with a white picket fence.

It was a warm June day in 1995 when I met him. There he was, asking if I wanted to join him for dinner. I hesitated, only saying yes because I knew my cousin had a crush on him, and she was standing right there. I looked at my cousin. She spoke up and encouraged me to go.

Dinner turned into another date for dinner and a movie. After our first date, I returned to where I was living only to find out that everyone was moving out and I was now homeless.

That turned into me moving in with him after the dinner and movie. I had known him for a long time prior to this, and all I could think of in that moment was how I needed a place to live.

Since he was thirteen years older than me, I looked at it as if he had everything together. He was romantic, caring, and concerned. These were things I always imagined I would find in a man. At the same time, I was scared about this move because we had only been on one date and I didn't want to become a live-in sex arrangement for him. He reassured me that he would not do anything until I was comfortable. So that next weekend, I moved in.

Things were great in the beginning of our relationship. We very seldom fought. He was the one! He loved me, and I loved him. About six months after I had moved in, we got married. At eighteen, I had our daughter and five years later, our son. I was living as close to my white-picket-fence dream life as possible.

My first clue that something was wrong should have been that week before the wedding. I ended up with a migraine and suffered up until three days before we were supposed to fly out. I asked him to take me to the hospital, and after getting a shot from the doctor, all I remember is waking up at my mom's house—the shot had knocked me out. Here I was about to get married, and my mom was taking care of me instead of my soon-to-be husband.

I eventually came to realize those times we seldom fought were not a good thing. It really meant I was holding everything in. He was a womanizer. We would go places, and he liked women to look at him. He was overly friendly with them. I hated confrontation and didn't want to fight, so I didn't really say much. I just kind of let it go.

I had started shopping uncontrollably and hiding the fact that I was spending tons of money. This created more tension in our relationship. I found myself having to get a job to pay off the debt I had placed on our family. I decided to buckle down and get my career together as an emergency medical technician.

My job as an EMT required me to work the nightshift. My husband did not like this. It created even more stress in our relationship. It reached the point that I didn't even want to be at home—all I wanted to do was go to work so I didn't have to be around him.

As I sat snacking and watching football in my favourite spot, he approached me. His words rang loud and painful—he wanted a divorce! I was devastated. My children could hear what was going on through the walls of their bedroom, and this is how they found out we were getting divorced.

That night, I found myself alone in bed, crying uncontrollably. I stayed up all night crying, trying to figure out ways to make this work. I didn't want my children to go through this. This couldn't be happening. I didn't want a divorce. I wanted my white picket fence life!

The next morning, when he came to the room to get his clothes for work, I begged and pleaded with him not to do this. But he told me it was already done.

I had two days to find a place to live. Every time I called him, I could feel him cringe. I would be his third divorce. He kept me even further than arms distance away from him. However, up until the day we went to the courthouse to finalize the divorce papers, I kept thinking it would work out. It would all be alright. This is not going to happen. He is going to change his mind. I was wrong. And he didn't waste any time sharing his life with his new girlfriend.

Here I was, a single mom, divorced, and in pain. It was like a whirlwind for me. But life didn't remain in this space forever.

It took a while to heal the relationship with my ex-husband. We both came to the agreement that we needed to continue a civil relationship so it would cause less impact on our children. We learned to communicate and express what we needed when it came to our children. There are times now that we even have breakfast together and our families mingle and get along.

I learned to heal and work through things that happened in my life. I knew that I had a greater purpose. To me, at the time, I knew that main purpose was to help others. I knew God would provide what I needed, and I would find that white-picket-fence love.

On November 27, 2011, I met my knight in shining armour. In the back of my mind, I had thought he would just leave me anyway, it was always when he would leave not if he was going to leave. This was engrained in my thought patterns but was not necessarily the truth. I had to let go of that expectation and let love find a home in my heart.

We were married in 2013. I had found it—real, true love. He was exactly what I had been looking for. He truly cared for me. Even though I knew this man and marriage was different, it took me a long time to really open up my heart and trust.

In fact, if I am being honest, it took me up to the last couple of months, here in 2014, that I feel comfortable saying he is not going to do anything behind my back. My new husband embraced me in love and helped me to overcome many hurtful things that lay within me. Through his love, I've learned so much.

One morning, I woke up feeling so sad. Why was I sad? I mean, I had married the man of my dreams—a true knight in shining armour. I had my white-picket-fence life. My husband, even though he was overseas, was working hard to support our family. But I found myself crying alone, not knowing why.

I called everyone I usually reached out to, only to find that none of them could speak with me in that moment. Talking to God was all I could do. I really just felt like I needed to get this stuff off my chest and just talk to someone.

That day, I was to meet someone for coffee. She could tell I had been crying and asked me if I needed to talk. As we talked, we went to have lunch and that's when my life changed again. She began to tell me about a nonprofit group she belonged to, and it was in that moment I knew my purpose.

Knowing what it was like to have my husband deployed, I wanted to start a nonprofit for women of military men. Not only was I sitting with the woman I had met for coffee but the woman who had started the nonprofit also joined us.

With my business experience, and with the amazing people I had met in Arizona, I knew it was time to start a nonprofit organization to support the families who have been affected by the war on terrorism. I now realized what I was put on this planet for. At thirty-eight years old, I felt complete with a sense of purpose. For the first time in my life, I am actually living my dream!

COMPILED by **KRISTY-LEA TRITZ**

Jeanette MacDonald

Jeanette MacDonald has worked with children, in many capacities, for over twenty years of her life. As a result, children's imaginations and their honest art have always been a source of fascination and inspiration for her. Lately, she has been using her own whimsical art to connect to her innocence and explore her life from this more simplistic perspective. She is presently semi-retired and pursuing her passion as a visual artist/illustrator and writer. It is her greatest wish that her art and writing may somehow assist others in finding their own childlike joy and inspiration.

www.jeanettemacdonaldart.com
info@jeanettemacdonaldart.com
facebook.com/jeanettemacdonaldart
twitter.com/jenmacart

COMPILED by **KRISTY-LEA TRITZ**

Chapter 14

OVER THE CLIFF OF LIFE: CLIMBING TO THE TOP ENOUGH!

Jeanette MacDonald

Alcohol and depression claimed my dad at the young age of forty-nine. He was a gregarious, talented, beautiful man who never knew he was enough. He spent his life searching for someone or something to show him that he was. On October 18, 1988, he got drunk for the last time, walked home across a train trestle, and fell to his death on the bridge below. I lost my dad that sad day without realizing that indeed he was enough.

Twelve years ago, my life was a big hot mess. I was drinking a lot! I felt like such a waste and disappointment to everyone, including myself. I said a little prayer for God to help me find my way. I had a vision of me as a tiny boat, lost in a stormy sea, violently tossed to and fro. I knew I would sink if something did not give.

I longed to somehow leave a legacy for my family. I wanted to make them proud of me. I had spent so many years trying to overcompensate to my children for what I thought were my shortcomings that I forgot to forgive myself and see all of the things I did right.

My whole life has been an anthology of survival stories. All of my stories add up to the whole of who I am and who I am becoming. When I was a small child, my dad's truck broke down on a snowy road in the frigid winter of Alberta. My dad left my sister Julie and I alone in the truck while he went for help. By the time he returned, both of us had pneumonia

When I was very young, I was cared for by someone who sexually abused me. At times, I had to care for my sister and would miss school doing parental duties, including cooking and cleaning. I never really had a chance to be a child. I felt it was robbed from me.

By the time I was fifteen, my mother had kicked me out of the house. I was terrified and just wanted my mother to ask me to come home. Instead, I left on a bus to go 497 miles away, to survive on my own.

At seventeen years old, I became pregnant. I grew up with my children. It was a harsh life. I felt alone, abandoned, and found it difficult to cope with daily life.

On August 11, 1994 in British Columbia, with my new puppy in the car, on my way to pick up my children, I felt happy. As I approached the summit on the logging road with its sharp switchback, my steering did not work. I slammed my foot on the brake. The car slid over a seven-hundred-foot cliff. I remember thinking, as the car violently crashed and rolled, that this was it! I could hear the puppy bouncing around the interior like she was a pinball.

I had no idea how far down the bottom was. I was driving a soft top Geo Tracker at the time. With a violent jolt, the crashing and tumbling came to an abrupt stop.

The car was finally still! I had been shaken so badly that everything looked as if I were seeing it through water. I knew that if I was to survive this crash, I needed to get myself back up to the road, so I undid my seatbelt and climbed out the smashed window.

On the passenger side of my car, the safety bar had come down like a sword into the passenger seat. If there had been a passenger, they would have been killed. The car looked like a crumpled beer can someone had thrown off the side of the cliff.

Looking up, I tried to get my bearings. The car had come to rest in a rocky dried-up creek bed, cliffs on both sides. I intuitively started climbing the cliff, facing the direction I thought would take me back to the road. I climbed and climbed, yelling for help as I did. I prayed to my dad to help me. I prayed to God. And I cried and I climbed.

On my climb, I saw that little blonde puppy huddled in a ball. Miraculously, she was still alive. I cried as I passed her, apologizing profusely for not having what it took to pick her up and carry her along with me. I knew it was going to take everything I had if I was to stand a chance at surviving this.

I did not think I had it in me to climb anymore. It was much too steep. I was in so much pain. Picking up a branch, I waved it up at the road above, thinking if someone passed by, they might be able to see it. I had to get up that last five feet or I would die.

By this time, I knew my back was broken. Every move was accompanied by a sharp shooting pain, and with it I saw a bright yellow streak of colour. I remember thinking that pain actually had a colour. I saw a Scottish broom growing, and I knew broom had a strong root system. So I grabbed that broom and hoisted myself up onto the logging road edge. It was all I could do to just get there. I laid there in a heap on top of a bed of sharp rocks.

As I lay on the side of that road twenty years ago, I thought about all the wild animals—bears and cougars—that might like to find this bloody mess of a helpless woman I was. Knowing the road was not well-traveled, I was terrified as I waited for a car to come along.

Forty-five minutes later, a car came around the bend. I saw the look on the passenger's face as they drove by me. They looked like they were watching a horror movie. I thought, "They are going to drive right by me."

Finally, they stopped. Two guys got out. The taller of the two asked me what had happened. I told them that I was in a car accident. Confused, they asked me where my car was. I pointed to the side of the cliff. Looking down the cliff, they said, "Holy shit!"

They could not believe it. You have to imagine what I must have looked like to them. I was covered in blood and had pieces of branches and glass all through my hair. I was wearing jean shorts and a tank top, revealing all the bruises that were beginning to take form.

When they first spotted me, they thought I might die, and that somehow they would be accused of doing that to me. The one fellow, who looked more fit, used ropes to climb down the cliff. He found the puppy and brought her up with him. Leaving me on the side of the road, they drove back the half hour to report the accident and get me some help, taking my puppy with them.

Before long, another car came by with a family in it. I had

been so afraid on the side of the road. This kind family stayed with me until the emergency vehicles and a helicopter arrived to take me.

I survived, and I came to know that I am enough—without an elixir. I am enough with all of my flaws. I am beautiful because of the fact that I fall. I am okay when I stutter. I am all right when I do not appear beautiful to everyone. You are—we all are—beautiful creations of God's imagination. Life is an amazing gift. One that I learned is definitely worth climbing life's steep cliffs.

I know how hard it can be to let go of the idea that we need to appear perfect. I am not sure where we get the idea that we are supposed to be perfect in the first place. Who gets to decide what perfection looks like anyway? Life is about the struggles. It is about going through them, learning about our humanness through them, and coming out the other side a more whole, complete, and real person.

Lately, I have begun to find my true voice through painting, blogging, and writing. I feel like I have found the real me for the first time. How did I find me? I found me by letting go of what I thought I was. I thought I was all those old painful stories. I thought they defined me. But I have come to realize I am not suffering. I am joy! You are too! Embrace life—you are enough!

COMPILED by **KRISTY-LEA TRITZ**

Jeannine Riant

Jeannine Riant guides women to find inner peace by helping them discover and embrace their personal inner support system, allowing them to be exactly where they are in that precise moment. Known for her soothing voice and compassion, she exudes positive energy, has a smile that is contagious, and an electric energy that draws people to her as she facilitates women to release what no longer serves them. Jeannine offers strategies and techniques that are unique to the client, moving them away from a confused and overwhelmed mind, back into their body, as they dive deep into clarity and focus within.

www.fundamentalfocusing.com
www.focuspointacademy.com
jeannineriant@gmail.com
facebook.com/fundamentalfocusing
twitter.com/focusingpointsca
ca.linkedin.com/pub/jeannine-riant/11/133/359/en

Chapter 15

I GOT MARRIED TWICE...TO THE SAME MAN!

Jeannine Riant

In 2006, my husband turned to me in bed with these haunting words: "I don't love you anymore." All I could do was turn my back to him, unable to say a word (or sleep through the night!) as I connected with a deep knowing of where we were headed. I felt lifeless.

It was on that night, three days after New Year's Eve, that I became a victim. I questioned, "How did we get to this point? Why did this happen? What did I do wrong?" Then I quickly wondered who else was involved. Why were we going through this?

I remember it well. The week was one of frustrations, overwhelm, and not knowing where or who to turn to. My imagination and inner voice started to get the best of me, as I couldn't see the full picture. I pointed the finger of blame. I felt angry and sorry for myself because of the situation I was in. I asked myself over and over again, "Why was I staying in an unhappy marriage anyways?"

I went to my friend's house down the road and told her: "Well, it looks like I am going to be a single mom!" She gave me a funny look and handed me a glass of wine! Although the wine helped, the conversation that followed was much more supportive.

I arrived home that evening at 11:00 p.m. to my husband

asking me, "Where were you? I thought we were going to talk." In his mind, he was ready for conversation. I, on the other hand, wasn't prepared for this. He hadn't told me we were going to have a "conversation." I took a deep breath and took a seat. He started the conversation with, "How did we get to where we are, and where do we go from here?"

The same questions were going through his mind, just as they had been running through mine. We sat and talked. He kept telling me, "I don't love you anymore." I could only respond, "Do what you need to do, but know that you have to leave the house if we're done." I felt alone, hurt, angry, and betrayed. Mixed emotions were running through my body. Do I accept it as it is and close the door? Do I try to make it work for the sake of the kids? Do I convince and beg him to come back, or do I let things unfold as they should, trying to keep sane through it all?

In my mind and my heart, I couldn't have him staying with me in "our" house, having meals with us, pretending to be a happy family. I couldn't have him continuing with our girls in a daily routine as if nothing happened. So the following day I asked him to leave.

When we ask for guidance—sometimes without even knowing we are asking for guidance—it's amazing what happens. That next day, the truck broke down. Unfortunately, the part he needed to fix it wouldn't be in the shop for a week. A WEEK! He was going to have to stay in our home for a week. (But definitely not in the same bed!)

A couple of days later, I went to my massage therapist— not for a massage but for a talk. This talk was about to change my whole outlook. I explained to him what happened. He simply asked, "Is there a place in your heart for forgiveness?" I replied, "Yes, I feel there's something inside of me that still loves him." I felt there was hope but I didn't know what he was thinking. I left his office with this statement in my mind about my marriage: "My door is still open but not forever. I can't go back to what was. We need to move forward from here."

This thought kept resonating with me. I still had this feeling in the bottom of my belly there was still space to love him and forgiveness was possible.

A week passed. Our story began to unfold. Together, we stopped the facade and spoke our "superficial" truth. We communicated how we felt, to the best of our ability at that point, and tried to figure out what the next steps would be. By the end of the week, he was leaving. Even with this knowing, there was a glimmer of hope within me. I listened to it. I kept the thought—maybe there would be more to our story.

The next Friday night, I came home late again. I was staying away as much as possible so that I wouldn't have to face him. It was hard to come home and see him there, knowing he wanted to leave. I noticed on this night that something had shifted in him. A conversation he had, a thought he had, a moment of regrouping and re-evaluating —I don't know to this day what transpired. He took me in his arms and said, "We need to talk." I hesitated but accepted the invitation.

We started to talk, I mean really talk. Not the superficial talk we had become accustomed to, but the real talk we did not want to face, the kind that left you open and vulnerable.

We came face to face with our fears, our emotions, our wants, needs, and compromises. We spoke of how we felt, where we were, what we needed and wanted. We each spoke of what we needed to move ahead to make this work —if being together was what we both wanted in the end.

What shifted things? What made things real and down to earth in order for me to able to make a decision that would create a better relationship? Going from what was to what was about to be? In my eyes, there were a few life lessons that enabled me to do so.

First, I stopped being a victim, and I started communicating my needs! I owned up to my half of the story. When I left my massage therapist's office and decided I had the openness to forgive, I also realized I had to accept it took two to tango. And if we were where we were, in this precise moment, it wasn't all because of him; I also had something to do with it.

Once I took a deeper look down the road, I quickly realized I had been angry for two years prior to this wall crumbling in front of me. I was not laughing anymore. I was upset and giving a whole lot of the "silent treatment" for days! It was not a healthy living space. I wasn't enjoying my children, as I did not have the energy to play and be present with them. Sex for me became a thing of the past. I didn't want him to even touch me.

I realized I had to take ownership for the "why we were where we were" and not fall into the trap of the blame game. That's easier said than done, but life flows so much smoother without the blame game.

Secondly, I realized I needed to take some "me time." For

me, it meant I literally had to take time for me. I had to be the person who figured me out, who got in tune with who I was and who I wanted to be. I had to change me... to be a better me, a better mom, and a better wife. With this came a whole lot of other things. With it came judgment—from me, and from my mother, friends, and colleagues. I felt people look at me and talk to me differently. Some even said, "You're so selfish!" when I would tell them I was going to take some time away from the family to go to a weekend retreat, or when I told them I was going away with my husband. No phone, no kids, no distractions as we figured out what our next steps were.

When I would hear those words, "You're so selfish!" I would second guess myself. I would go back into deep thought, into that place where I would doubt and question what I was doing. I would let my little voice become the commanding voice and sometimes wonder if I was just losing it!

In the end, I wasn't losing it. I was just going through the motions of what it is to face my own wall, to watch it crumble, and then have to break through it in order for it not to build itself up again.

We did not physically remarry; however, in my mind we did. I found my first true love, the one I had lost somehow along the way, through the chaos and busyness of life! Instead of letting life take ahold of me, I started truly living life—with my husband once again.

COMPILED by **KRISTY-LEA TRITZ**

Jenni Ryan

Jenni Ryan is a network marketing trainer, coach, and team leader. Jenni spends her time building and helping her team to become successful, as well as doing training that helps anyone in any company. Jenni has had a decade of experience in network marketing and has found her passion in this industry. Jenni's WHY is to take a stand for others so that they may overcome and truly shine. When Jenni is not working and traveling, she enjoys snow skiing and having fun.

www.jenniryan.com
facebook.com/fjenniryanfb
youtube.com/meetjenniryan
au.linkedin.com/in/whoisjenniryan

COMPILED by **KRISTY-LEA TRITZ**

Chapter 16

BLACK SHEEP: TURNING YOUR PAIN INTO YOUR PASSION

Jenni Ryan

I remember growing up and being the different one—the black sheep in the family. It made me feel like I wasn't good enough. It created within me a sense of misplacement in my life, where I really struggled to identify with the people around me.

My sisters were both A grade students. I was a freethinker, one who didn't like to be bound by rules. I was too busy daydreaming and getting in trouble in class for not listening, talking too much, and being distracted. It cemented that feeling that I was different.

My childhood was not the happiest or easiest. After going through my parents' divorce, which left me feeling sad, confused, emotional, and lost, I lived with my two sisters and my mum. I don't even remember huge chunks of my childhood, possibly as parts of it were too painful and have been subconsciously blocked out. Eventually, I came to realize, through this part of my life, that everything happens for a reason. What I went through in my childhood has helped to shape who I am today.

I barely remember my dad living with us. However, I do remember a couple of traumatic experiences. When I was eighteen months old, my mum was in the hospital having my sister. My dad was taking care of me while she was in the hospital. He didn't know how to change my nappy (diaper). Instead of changing my nappy, he took me outside, shook it off me, and hosed me down. I guess he just did the best he knew.

When I was ten years old, I remember events taking place that left me feeling like I should have done more to protect my mum so she didn't have to suffer and feel the way she did. My dad had a bad temper and was not equipped to deal with kids.

My parents divorced when I was about eleven years old, and I had to spend every second weekend going to my dad's house. I would stand at the front door screaming because I did not want to go. I don't exactly remember why, other than I didn't feel safe or happy about it.

Growing up, I always felt like I wasn't good enough, partly because of the family breakdown and partly because I was the different one. I was not the academic who thrived on studying.

In my early twenties, I had a short stint in the corporate world in a media buying agency. I felt completely out of place. All it took was one person to make the work environment difficult. I'd find I couldn't stand up to them and prove my worth. I was still that vulnerable little girl who felt trapped and unable to speak up.

At the age of twenty-two, I threw it all in and moved to a ski resort where I spent the next eight years in between various things, enjoying life. I worked hard and partied hard. Life was like a dream, a fairy tale. I was independent and free. Roaming around and doing whatever I wanted.

Over these years, I became a lot more street smart because I was traveling and meeting so many different people from all walks of life.

Eventually I realized that I had to think more long-term instead of living the way I was. I needed to do something to settle down. After a few years working in a remote mining town in Western Australia, I met my husband and moved back to Melbourne, where we had two kids.

After my first child was born, I knew I absolutely could not just sit at home and be a stay-at-home mum. I needed something else. However, I knew I didn't want to work for someone else, so I began a search for my calling. I searched the Internet for weeks until I found an opportunity to work from home.

This was the beginning of my journey into network marketing, into the place where I would find my purpose. I started off wide-eyed and overambitious, believing I was going to be rich in a very short space of time. However, that was not the case. I struggled for years. But resilience and persistence was on my side. I had something to prove to myself and to everyone else. I wanted to prove to myself that I was worthy and capable of impacting others in a positive way. I certainly wasn't just going to sit in a corner and let life beat me.

In network marketing, I discovered a profession where I was able to make an impact in the world. This made me feel as if I had found my life's purpose, and this was the vehicle where I could achieve that.

It is a profession where a very high percentage of people fail, because it is so easy to get into and also so easy to get out of. Most people don't have the persistence or the vision to keep pushing through all the obstacles and challenges that they face as they strive to become the best and build a team of thousands.

If you have nothing else but persistence, you will overcome everything and create the results you want. Without persistence, you will never get results in anything. Just like a child learning to walk, it takes many failures and many challenges to overcome and finally be able to say you did it. Just like it took me years to overcome and work through what happened in my childhood, I knew it would take that same dedication and persistence to be a successful entrepreneur.

Leadership from the Heart

It took me years of struggling and watching others struggle to realize that my goals were bigger than just me making money and becoming successful. My heart was really driven by helping others overcome so that they could live their life to their highest potential.

I felt a strong calling to be someone that was known as authentic, honest, and a voice of reason in an industry that is often filled with hype and untruth of making it look easy. I tell it like it is. I try to shine the light for people who have the drive but lack the belief in themselves. I do this so that they can overcome and truly shine just like I was able to.

If it wasn't for the heartbreak in my childhood, and the feelings of not being good enough, perhaps I would not have grown to be so passionate about taking a stand for others. I believe that everyone—no matter what their story—has the ability to draw from their past to fuel their future success.

Personal development over those ten years has played a huge part in discovering who I am, helping me to overcome and allowing me to discover my role as a leader and how I can impact others through that leadership. Most of my training is focused on marketing and mindset. I believe wholeheartedly that success is 90 percent mindset. No matter how talented or skilled you are, without the right mindset, you will continue to struggle.

5 Tips to Overcome Failure and Create Successful Leadership

Self-belief: Most people don't want to hear it or believe it, but daily mindset training with personal development is the key to your success. When you believe in yourself and what you are doing this creates a much stronger pull toward your vision and goals. Others around you will see and feel this.

Self-leadership: Self-leadership is the discipline of being able to lead yourself through obstacles and challenges, no matter what you are feeling, so that you may in turn lead others. Learning how to overcome these obstacles in your life will help you teach others how to do the same.

Vision: Clarity of your vision is what will help you persevere through everything. You need to be emotionally connected to your vision, and it has to be crystal clear. When you focus on making an impact on others, people will start to believe what you believe and share in your vision, which will help them find their own.

Heart: You must have a heart for others. Your goals must be way bigger than just making money or having material things in life. You get the privilege and ability to make choices that will impact the world on a larger scale. It's always much more fulfilling when it's about impacting others.

Passion: You have to believe 100 percent in what you do and be passionate about what you do. It is very hard to keep going and persevere if you are not passionate about what you do. When you are passionate, it fuels your drive.

Jennifer Gardner

Jennifer Gardner, LMT, is an expert JFB myofascial release therapist, a craniosacral therapist, a Reiki master, an energy worker, a teacher, a student, an empath, a mom, an introvert, an aromatherapist, and an intuitive facilitator of the healing process. She spent much of her life living by others' rules, which was the root cause of her anxiety and depression. Now she lives by her own rules. She is continually discovering a new sense of health, happiness, calm, and peace. Jennifer is the owner and sole practitioner at Massagology, LLC, where she facilitates healing and transformations to healthier lifestyles.

www.massagology.net

jennifer@massagology.net

facebook.com/pages/massagology-LLC/135406639808392

www.linkedin.com/pub/jennifer-gardner/7/32a/6ba

COMPILED by **KRISTY-LEA TRITZ**

Chapter 17

LOSS: FINDING STRENGTH THROUGH GRIEF

Jennifer Gardner

I stood in the vestibule of the church looking at his face over the coffin positioned between us. I didn't know who he was, so I tried to avoid eye contact.

My mother was in that coffin. I didn't want him to look at me. I didn't want anyone to look at me. I was motherless. Half of an orphan. I was ashamed. He kept looking at me, and I just wanted him to stop staring. He was close to my age, but I knew that he had a mother. I knew he only volunteered to be an altar boy at my mom's funeral to get out of school, and now he was standing there feeling sorry for me. I stood out. Like I had a neon sign over my head; "Hey! Look at the motherless daughter!"

My dead mother was my scarlet letter, prompting an endless line of friends, relatives, neighbours, and nibshitters to deliver looks of pity, fabricated hugs, and empty condolences in my ear.

I was numb. After days of receiving guests while standing beside my mother's embalmed, emaciated, wigged corpse, I was numb. Standing there over her coffin, I couldn't remember if we were going into the church for mass or leaving the church to go to the grave site for her burial. I just remember that altar boy. The one who kept staring at me. I didn't want to know what he really thought of me, but I imagined it was bad.

Looking back, I don't remember the rest of my 8th grade year.

I had known for months that my mom was not going to survive the cancer, and I was prepared for her death. For nearly a year I had gone to great lengths to distance myself from her. I had made a conscious choice not to care. If I didn't care, it wouldn't hurt when she died. Right?

I would erupt in outbursts of anger and tell her that I hated her just to prove to myself and to everyone else that this was not going to affect me. I tried to focus on my friends at school in an attempt to be normal. I wanted to fit in with the normal crowd. I was a loud, obnoxious pre-teen thinking this would mask the pain I faced at home.

I didn't want anyone to know that my life at home sometimes meant I was helping Mom off of the floor in the bathroom after a bout of vomiting following a chemotherapy treatment. I didn't want anyone to know that I knew what chemotherapy vomit looked and smelled like. I didn't want anyone to know that we had vials of morphine in the medicine cabinet. I didn't want anyone to know that I bought my mom flannel pyjamas for Christmas because she didn't wear normal clothes anymore. I just wanted to be a normal, boy-crazy, 13-year-old girl like the rest of my friends.

The plan failed, and it failed miserably. My attempts to distance myself from her, to hate her so her imminent death wouldn't hurt me, didn't work. I was not prepared for the physical pain that seared through my body when the hospital called to tell us she had passed. In that instant, I knew I had let her down. I had failed her as a daughter. I did everything wrong leading up to this moment, but it took this moment for me to realize it. There were no do-overs. It was too late. She died alone in the hospital, and I had betrayed her in the worst way.

I looked around and realized I was at the home of my dad's girlfriend when my mother died. And my mom knew it. She was dead. How could she not know at that point? I imagined her reaching out to me when she died only to discover where I was. In death, I was transparent to her. She could see right through the walls I had carefully constructed, and what she saw was disappointing. I knew it.

For years afterwards, I lived the many faces of grief. I wished it had been me that died instead of my mother. I pleaded with the god who wasn't there to bring her back and take me instead. When I was angry with my father, I would secretly wish it had been him who had passed instead of my mother.

My anger spewed and blame for her death passed from the hospital, to my father, and eventually targeted myself. It was my fault. I convinced myself that she didn't love me enough to want to live, so she chose to give up. I wasn't good enough, and I got exactly what I deserved for being such a horrible daughter.

The recurring nightmares were confirmation for me that it was my fault. On and off for several years, mom would appear in my dreams. She would be happy, healthy, and alive. When I would approach her to tell her how much I had missed her and how happy I was to see her again, she would look at me with disgust and loathing on her face. She would say, "I don't know you. Leave me alone." In several of these dreams, she would threaten to call security or have me arrested. I would wake in tears, devastated. In death, she disowned me. She knew the truth about me that I tried to hide from the world, and I deserved her disdain.

Over the years, the grief continued to rear its head in ugly ways. My attempts to hide from the world became increasingly desperate. In high school and college, I used diet pills and laxatives to mitigate the loathing I felt for my body. I convinced myself that being beautiful on the outside would disguise the ugliness inside.

To cope with social situations, I turned to alcohol and superficial relationships built on little more than convenience and sex. When conflict arose or commitment was mentioned, I moved on to the next passing relationship. I was a master at avoidance. I watched hours of television every day. It was easy for me to get caught up in the drama of other people's lives, fiction or otherwise; it's how I avoided my own.

Then a career change changed my life. Not just my professional life, but my whole being. After becoming a massage therapist, I attended a continuing education class that planted the seeds of healing. This wasn't just healing on the surface, but a deep healing of the soul.

I listened to others emote. Without fear, they allowed their emotions to rise to the surface and be released. This was eye opening for me. And scary! These classes were teaching me a form of bodywork that was different than the massage I had learned in school. It encompassed healing on multiple levels, not just healing of the physical body.

Despite my doubts and to my surprise, I was finally

healing from my grief by allowing myself to express the emotions that I had bottled-up most of my life. I was learning to emote in a healthy way. I was learning to experience my emotions without letting my emotions control my behaviours. Slowly I was becoming less loathsome.

I stopped avoiding the grief and met it head-on. Turns out, it was okay for me to feel anger, guilt, and shame; that's part of the process. It was okay that I felt anger toward others and that my mind tried to find fault and assign blame. That is also part of the process. It was okay to feel sad, and it was okay to cry. Numbing and avoiding the pain made the process worse and led me to dysfunctional and self-destructive behaviours. I stopped comparing my experience with the experiences of others. I accepted that my grieving process is unique to me, and there is no standard amount of time allotted for me to grieve.

The ugliness I saw inside of myself was nothing more than emotions I suppressed and refused to express. What I had imagined that altar boy saw was just that, my imagination.

I kept my emotions hidden for years before allowing them to surface out of fear that others would see the same ugliness I did. My dysfunctional behaviours were a facade, an attempt to keep these emotions hidden from the rest of the world. My need to keep them hidden was my fear of being vulnerable.

The throes of grief sent me into a state of vulnerability with which I was not comfortable nor did I know how to handle. An important part of my healing process has been being okay with being alone and being silent. Sitting alone in silence for hours has helped me to connect with myself. I already know the answers, and I'm healing myself by tapping into that knowledge through my inner-connection.

Jenny Call

Jenny Call is a myofascial release therapist, specializing in women's prenatal health, and working with clients suffering from chronic undiagnosed pain. Her motto is to "get clients off her table and living their life." Jenny is a single mother who enjoys spending time with her two beautiful daughters, spending time with friends and family, and being active outdoors.

www.jennycallmyofascialrelease.com
mfrjenny@gmail.com
facebook.com/jennyhanselcallcmt

COMPILED by **KRISTY-LEA TRITZ**

Chapter 18

STILL SMALL VOICE: LIVING LIFE AS IT WAS MEANT TO BE!

Jenny Call

It was the summer of 2007. I was five months pregnant with my first daughter, Abby. My husband and I had gotten into a fight, and that was the first time those words ever came out of my mouth—"I want a divorce."

I attributed this to my hormonal state, apologized a thousand times, and life went on. Yes, life went on as it normally did. I went on to have two healthy daughters, and life as I knew it was very good. However, I was not happy. At all.

As my daughters began to grow and get older, I had experienced what many may call my awakening. I knew there was more for me out there. Many things led up to the end of my marriage. But, if I were honest, I would realize that I was never truly happy in my marriage to begin with.

Sure, I was comfortable, financially secure, had a beautiful home, two beautiful/healthy/happy daughters—I had it all! Except for the love I so desired, and the opportunity to pursue my purpose—whatever that was.

When I was growing up, all I was ever told to do was study hard, go to college, get a degree, get a job that paid well—one that offered good health insurance—and marry a man who could support my love for horses. Never, ever was

I encouraged to find what I wanted to do in life and pursue what I was passionate about. I had no clue what I was doing.

I felt like I floated through college without an idea as to what my future held for me, or what I wanted to do. I graduated from college and got a job working in research at a large pharmaceutical company. Soon after I began working there, I met my future husband.

Not knowing anything about love, or what love truly meant to me, I moved deeper into my relationship. We moved in together, and three years into our relationship we were married. Three months after getting married, I became pregnant with our first daughter. About a year and a half later, I became pregnant with my second daughter.

Throughout the course of our relationship, I began to notice how our communication was disintegrating. I became very resentful and angry all the time. I became hurtful and mean and not the person I knew I was. I lost myself in my relationship, wanting to please others first and not myself.

In April 2011, I began experiencing major debilitating anxiety attacks. I had no clue why this was happening. My body seemed to be reacting to something that was happening in my life, something I was ignoring. It was at the same time we were experiencing major shifts in our physical environment, choosing to move to a new house and start anew.

This major transition increased my anxiety. I was unable to control what was happening to my body and began taking anxiety medication, adding them to the antidepressants I had been taking for years. As I continued through my path, I realized traditional therapy was not something that would help me.

I began working with a life coach. Knowing this work was more progressive and forward-moving, I felt like I was moving in the right direction. I realized I was not living my purpose. Once I was able to say those words—I'm not living my purpose—it took a huge load off my shoulders. My coach and I continued to work together. At this point, I began to include my husband in my sessions.

As my coaching sessions progressed, I began to acknowledge that I did not want to be married to my husband any longer. This was devastating to me! However, I had to acknowledge it was the truth. Once the truth came out, I felt such relief. The hardest part was telling my husband that I did not want to be married anymore. I assured him it was not from any wrongdoing or cheating. It was truly because I was finally starting to listen to myself— for the first time in my life.

It was at a combined birthday party for my two and four– year-old that I chose to announce to my family and friends that my husband and I were separating. Why then? Why did I feel so relieved, so happy? I asked myself these questions, and the answer for me was I was so unhappy in the rest of my life that it was a relief to announce we were separating.

I moved out of the house we had just moved into and went back to our house in Santa Cruz. It was difficult leaving my young children, especially leaving them with my husband, who was so distraught he was barely able to care for himself—let alone two young girls.

I often wondered if we would have been married as long as we were if we didn't have the girls. I must have cried off and on for the better part of two years, questioning myself. What am I doing? Why am I doing this to myself, my family?

For years, my husband blamed me for breaking up our family. Years! However, I did not see it that way. I saw it as an opportunity for us to pursue our own individual happiness in relationships, in life, and in work. I did not feel as though I was pursuing the work I was put here on this earth to do.

During the separation, I began to take courses at one of the local massage therapy schools. I knew I wanted to pursue a career and a life as a birth doula. I took the certification course but still thought there was something else I was meant to be doing. Something to bring me full circle.

I chose to pursue my own myofascial release therapy practice. I knew this was something I had always wanted to do. So I began taking the massage therapy classes to be able to attend the myofascial release therapy sessions that I was interested in. Starting my own practice was terrifying! What if I failed? I would only fail if I did not attempt to do what I was put here to do.

Jerri Eddington

Jerri Eddington, EdD, LICDC, OCPS, is the creator of Energy Connections and the co-creator of Lighten Up and Thrive. Lighten Up and Thrive! is a sacred vision of sharing our expertise and wisdom as transformational life coaches. We facilitate powerful, transformative programs so you can experience "joyful living for mind, body and soul." We embrace the mystery of ALL that YOU can be.

In addition to her energy/healing modalities, Jerri has thirty-six years' experience as an educator, counsellor, and coach. She lives with her husband, Bob, in the Phoenix, Arizona area.

Email: jerri@lightenupandthrive.com
Email: jerrieddington@gmail.com
Facebook (personal): http://www.facebook.com/jerri.eddington
FB (Energy Connections): http://www.facebook.com/DrJerri57
FB (Lighten Up and Thrive): https://www.facebook.com/lightenup.andthrive
Google +: https://plus.google.com/u/0/+JerriEddingtonEdD/posts
LinkedIn: http://www.linkedin.com/in/drjerrieddington
Skype: drjerri57
Twitter: https://twitter.com/DrJerri57
Website for Author Jerri Eddington: http://www.authordrjerrieddington.com
Website for Energy Connections: http://www.drjerrieddington.com
Website for Let Your Soul Shine: http://www.let-your-soul-shine.com
Website for Lighten Up and Thrive!:http://www.lightenupandthrive.com
YouTube: http://www.youtube.com/channel/UC_Wqxz9mCVufW1INuxo0C6Q

COMPILED by **KRISTY-LEA TRITZ**

Chapter 19

I BROKE THE SILENCE TO ALLOW HEALING TO BEGIN

Jerri Eddington

When I was about seven years old, I realized my dad had a drinking problem. I don't remember many times when my dad wasn't drinking.

Mom was forty-one years old and Dad was forty-five when I was born. We lived in an area called "The Bottoms" in Columbus, Ohio. My family is originally from Tennessee, they moved to Ohio before I was born, because dad lost his job. Dad had a milk truck route. He lost his job one day after having too much to drink. He'd driven into a group of cows, killing a few.

My mom's sister allowed my family of seven to live in her basement until my dad could find another job. Years later, at a family reunion, I heard that my mom almost left my dad when he lost his job. I got very excited... then I realized had she left, I wouldn't be here!

My dad worked second shift. He would go to the bar every night after work. Coming home, he would wake me up and be really hateful and argumentative. It was hard for me to focus at times in school because I was always tired.

School became a safe haven for me. I loved my second grade teacher, Mrs. Asbury. She was a strong, positive influence in my life. She is the reason I decided to become a teacher. I knew I wanted to help other kids the way she helped me. Around this same time period, my mom's church adopted a fundamentalist doctrine. I was living in a house with extremes of good and evil.

It was very confusing to live in my house. I made friends with people who had lots of siblings. I would go to my friend's house whenever I could. I was afraid to bring friends home because I never knew what I would find. I felt like I lived on a roller coaster... my feelings would go up and down. Extracurricular activities at school kept me very busy.

During the tenth grade, I met Terry. He was two years older than I. Both of Terry's parents were alcoholics. He acted as a main caregiver for his sister and three brothers.

One day, one of his brothers was missing. He called the police because he didn't know where his parents were. The police took all the children to the child protective agency. Terry and his oldest brother went to live with their aunt and uncle. His other siblings went to foster homes. Terry and I started dating and I became pregnant at fifteen years old. Terry graduated in June and we got married in July. I went from one crazy situation to another one.

In September, I talked to my principal about keeping up with my assignments. I was taking college prep classes since I was still planning on becoming a teacher. I was assigned a tutor. My son, Shawn, was born in October. My tutor stayed with me until the end of the semester. When I returned to school, I had enough credits to graduate high school a year early. I was ready to start college... but I didn't have any money.

Since I didn't get married until July, my dad claimed me

on his taxes. He made too much money for me to get any financial help. Towards the end of the school year, the principal made an announcement telling students who still needed financial assistance for college to report to a meeting in the auditorium.

Staff members from Ohio State University were there to talk about a new program, Freshman Foundation. The program was started to assist minority students. Since my parents were from Tennessee, I was coded as an Appalachian. This was a stretch... but I was provided the funds to attend college.

It was challenging juggling marriage, motherhood, and being a full-time student at seventeen years old. My whole world changed during my second quarter in college.

On February 1, my seventeen-year-old brother in-law was killed drinking and drag racing. Terry and I planned his funeral with no help from his parents. Three weeks later, my son died from complications of the flu. I was devastated. Four months later, I suffered a miscarriage. Terry's drinking increased, and our arguing and physical fighting increased too. Christmas that year was horrible.

I had three new nephews and a passed out husband on Christmas Eve. I was so sad and heart broken. It was a while before I could enjoy Christmas again.

My son, Marcus, was born two years later. I graduated college and started teaching at the junior high school I'd attended. My dad passed away suddenly after having a heart attack. My son, Jeremy, was born during my first full year of teaching. The stress of Terry's drinking was getting harder and harder to deal with. The arguing was having an impact on my sons, too.

My sister, Rose, was diagnosed with leukemia. She had five siblings, but no one was a match for her to have a bone marrow transplant. They did not have a national bone marrow bank at that time. My sister was dying. I realized I was dying too... in my marriage. After ten years, I got a divorce.

Soon I met Bob, my current husband. We will celebrate our thirtieth anniversary next year.

Five months before Bob and I were married, I took a class to help my students who were living in alcoholic homes. The first night of class, the teacher went over the syllabus. We were told we needed to look at our own alcohol use and the use within our family. I raised my hand to say I was here to help my students. I was told that in order to help others, we must look at our own use first!

Children of parents who abuse alcohol or other drugs run a higher risk of becoming abusers. I started a support group for students from alcoholic homes. There was a little girl in my first group whose father drank with my father. Her mother was a barmaid at the same bar. I was a homeschool community agent, which is similar to a counselling position. I created ten support groups with support from various community agencies.

I decided I wanted to help more students than just those in my school. Being a district drug/alcohol program coordinator allowed me to accomplish this goal. I created classes to teach school staff members how to start support groups in their own schools.

I spent many years burying the pain caused by my dad's drinking. I learned that to start recovering from the effects of growing up in an alcoholic family, you've got to walk through the pain—not around it, not under it, but through it. Children growing up in alcoholic homes live by three rules: 1) You don't talk about what is going on; 2) You don't share your feelings; 3) You don't trust. I have *consciously* been breaking these rules for many years as I reach out to help others.

I found an excellent resource for educators: *Children of Alcoholics: A Kit for Educators,* by the National Association for Children of Alcoholics. Research shows children who *survive* living in an alcoholic family have found one or two adults they can trust and who provide support to them over the years. Many times, the adult who helps them is a teacher. This was certainly true for me, starting in the second grade.

A tool shared in the *Kit for Educators*—which is called Seven Cs—is used to help young people understand they are not responsible for their parents' problems. Children need to know that it is not their fault when their parents drink too much and that they cannot control their parents' behaviour. They also should be shown that there are ways they can learn to deal with their parents' alcoholism.

For additional info, please check out this http://www.nacoa.org.

I also found Delores Curran's *Traits of a Healthy Family* very helpful in my family's recovery process. Her book shows how to evaluate your family's strengths and weaknesses, how to work on problem areas, and how to make your family healthier.

For help dealing with parental alcoholism, please check

out http://al-anon.org/for-alateen and http://www.adultchildren.org

Karen Packwood

Karen is an international author, clairvoyant/healer, and educator. She founded The Spirit Spa in 2014 to bring her work with and for Spirit to more people. She specializes in healing core wounds of the inner child by acting as a conduit between Spirit and the client, enabling a gentle and loving connection/transformation of the trauma and grief at the heart of each issue, successfully bringing about a renewed sense of empowerment and joy. Karen's work includes, amongst other things, in-depth readings with Spirit, Wise Wisdom vision quests, 101 mentoring/spiritual guidance, psychic surgery, and live retreats.

www.thespiritspa.international
karenpackwood@gmail.com
www.facebook.com/lovelyselfhealing & /karen.packwood1
twitter.com/karen_packwood
uk.linkedin.com/in/karenpackwood

COMPILED by **KRISTY-LEA TRITZ**

Chapter 20

TIME TO FORGIVE

Karen Packwood

I was twelve when I was first abandoned by my mother. I came home unexpectedly early from my Saturday job to discover suitcases piled up in the hallway of our home, my brother standing beside them. My mother was in my bedroom writing a letter on scented pink stationery. They both looked shocked to see me.

Almost immediately after my entrance, a taxi's horn blared outside. My mother instructed me to take her letter to my father in his office downtown. Her parting words, before turning me out of the house, were:

"No matter what happens, I'll always love you."

The taxi horn blasted again. I knew in that second my life had changed forever.

I hadn't walked very far up the gentle incline of our road when the taxi drove past me, the heads of my brother and mother just visible through the windows. Neither of them looked at me, their faces fixed firmly on the open road ahead of them. I watched as they disappeared out of sight, the letter clutched in my shaking hand, my stomach churning with nausea.

I managed a few more steps and then it happened. The shattering. The splintering. An internal cascade of my entire inner world. The collapse of my whole being. To the outside world, I wouldn't have looked a tiny bit different. But inside, I was broken to smithereens, like a porcelain doll dropped from a great height. My entire world of safety swept away in one fell swoop.

It doesn't take long for a child to take these events and internalize them in a very personal way. I can remember to this day what I was wearing—blue Wrangler jeans and a red T-shirt. I can remember how uncomfortable my body felt as I walked: ugly and fat. I remember the rage towards my mother erupting within, lasting for all of a few seconds before I had twisted and turned it around on myself.

In the short fifteen minute walk to my father's office, I had internalized these feelings about myself:

I'm hateful.

I don't belong.

I'm not special.

I'm fat.

I'm ugly.

I'm repulsive.

I'm not wanted.

I'm ridiculous.

I'm shameful.

I'm not loveable.

I don't deserve to be loved.

Of course, I wasn't aware of those feelings at the time. The splintering was succeeded by a deep numbing. I dutifully gave my father the letter, and then life entered a surreal world of silence and cover-up—the ultimate world of shame.

How could I tell my friends at school that my mother had left me? Left me! What a bad, hateful, terrible person I must be.

How could I even begin to admit to myself that I had been abandoned by the one person who was meant to be there for me through thick and thin? And, of course, there was the added horror that my brother was taken—chosen—whilst I was rejected.

Once rejected by your mother, you are left with just one resounding feeling: I am shit.

For many years, I lived with this feeling, acting it out and reinforcing it in a variety of ways, mostly in unhealthy relationships and self-destructive behavior. I spent years in therapy, working hard to reclaim my own sense of self-respect and love. But it's hard to do this once you've been rejected by the one person who was meant to create a foundational rock of safety and security in your life. It never dawned on me that it would happen once more, when I was aged forty-eight.

It was all brought to light again by a relationship I was in with a guy who was like an emotional yo-yo. One minute he loved me and wanted to be with me; the next he was backing off, ignoring me, shunning me, and claiming not to love me. One particular day, there was an event where he shunned me in an extraordinarily painful way, churning up so many latent feelings around the whole abandonment issue.

By this stage, my mum and I had seemed to reach a happier place in our relationship. She'd been an amazing support to me through some difficult times during the birth of my own daughter. I felt we'd moved on in a good way.

So, one day, shortly after these feelings had been churned up, I tried to have a conversation with her about why she'd left. I genuinely believed we were in a strong enough place to discuss the emotions around this whole experience in a mutually supportive manner, to come to a place of healing. I was aware I still had unresolved emotions that were spilling out into our relationship, bringing sadness to us both. I wasn't, however, prepared for the difficult conversation that was to ensue. I wasn't prepared for some of the shocking things she said to me, for her cold denial about so many of my own deeply painful and vivid memories.

The thing that hurt me the most, however, was that she seemed so unable to truly hear my pain or to understand my agony. At the time, it was excruciating. She did say she was sorry, but somehow, for me, that just didn't seem to be enough or even feel real. I was left, for a second time, feeling emotionally bereft. How on earth could I heal myself of these devastating feelings and beliefs? How on earth was I ever going to bring myself back into a place of wholeness?

After several months of continued rage erupting from nowhere and always directed at my mother, I made a discovery. Talking was obviously never going to heal these feelings. Screaming at my mother was clearly never going to bring any lightness to this dark, sad situation. There was something else going on, some other emotion attached to this story that I hadn't connected with fully. It was there beneath the rage, beneath the pain. Throbbing away.

One day, as I walked by my local canal under the stars in the moonlight, it came to me. The ultimate feeling nagging away, gnawing a hole in my heart.

Grief.

I had never allowed the little girl—who had suffered such a deep loss—to grieve. It wasn't that she needed to be heard by my mother, although that would be nice. It wasn't that she needed to be angry with others. Lord knows she had exhibited enough anger in her life to know that it only bought more pain and destruction to her and others.

No. What this little twelve–year-old needed was to be held in her grief. To be loved through it, tenderly and sweetly. And there was only one person capable of doing this. Me.

It couldn't be my mother. She had her own grief to deal with. This healing had to come from within myself. And so there, under the stars, I gave myself permission to enter into grief. Grief for that little girl's shock when she first saw those suitcases. For her excruciating heartache as her mum and brother drove out of sight. For her terror at the prospect of being alone in the world without a mother to guide her. And most of all, for the grief of holding such terribly wrong beliefs about herself for so long. She knew that it was time to stop believing that she was shit.

It was the depth of winter when I first connected consciously with my little twelve-year-old self, just before the Winter Equinox, when we celebrate the return of light to our days. And so it was that I decided to be mother to myself. Only I could possibly know what I needed to do or be in order to heal. I knew I needed time and space. I needed to be with nature. I needed silence. I needed peace—to be *with myself* and *for myself*.

I spent a lot of time walking. Early in the morning, I would take myself on dawn walks before the day broke, walking through the shadows of trees and hedges, watching the silhouettes of swans gliding past me, listening to the ducks washing themselves in the ice cold water.

I would walk in to the sunrise often, having my breath taken away by the sudden appearance of the golden sun blazing on the horizon. As I walked, I allowed this precious twelve-year-old within to speak with me, to share with me her sadness and pain.

I was the one who needed to hear her. I was the one who needed to listen. And I was the only one who could honour her needs. By these hedgerows and trees, as the birds began to sing their dawn chorus, I finally allowed her tears to fall.

And it was in this listening and hearing, this allowing and being, that she came back to life. No longer was she numb with trauma or wild with rage. No longer did she feel invisible or uncared for. No longer did she feel silenced or repressed. No longer did she feel ashamed or unloved. No.

She grew as we walked, this precious child. Each step bringing her to new life. Each step creating strength and courage. Each step bringing her back to what she had always been: a beautiful, sweet, and magnificent soul—as stunning, vibrant, and loving as the early morning sun in which she now walked, leaving the darkness far behind.

As she healed, she was able to hear, as if for the first time, the words of her mother that she knew were true. Only now could she truly believe them:

"*No matter what happens, I will always love you.*"

And she knew, without a shadow of a doubt, what her next step must be.

I must learn to forgive.

COMPILED by **KRISTY-LEA TRITZ**

Kris McLeod

Kris is a healer, coach, and writer with a background in natural health, science and education. She has a successful remedial massage and health coaching practice and is a business coach with Goddess Business School.

Kris is deeply passionate about coaching and helping people live better lives, and she believes that being empowered in your health, work, and life makes that experience richer. She loves to help her clients bring their health, business, wellbeing, and fun back into picture. She lives in Australia, in the beautiful Adelaide Hills, with her husband and fur-kids.

www.wellnesswonderwomen.com
kris@wellnesswonderwomen.com
facebook.com/wellnesswonderwomen

COMPILED by **KRISTY-LEA TRITZ**

Chapter 21

WRESTLING WITH HIGH ACHIEVEMENT: LEARNING TO BE GROUNDED IN SELF-CARE

Kris McLeod

To say that I fell for the "high achievement equals success" fallacy is an understatement! It went beyond the standard "be a good girl, get good grades, get a great job, and you'll be happy" myth—I took it to extremes.

I thought anything less than an "A" wasn't good enough; distinction or high distinction was the goal—even if I got stressed, even if I got sick. I placed my feelings of self-worth and value on those results. I ignored being sick and tired, and I thought the stress would be worth it in the end.

To add to the craziness, I thought I was playing the game really well!

By the time I was at university, I was juggling part-time work, full-time study, part-time massage classes, and a very full social life! Whenever anything extra cropped up, I thought I might crack. Argument with my boyfriend? Feeling overloaded! A personal crisis during exams? Meltdown! I set unrealistic goals, and because I was used to meeting them, I just kept pushing.

There was a time, in my final year of uni, that I realized, with a shock, I had just one day that month that I didn't have to be at work or study.

If someone needed me or a friend was upset, I just reprioritized. The guilt of saying no was more exhausting than the over-giving. I thought that if I could make everyone happy, I'd be happy. Good girls cared, good girls looked after others.

My eating was affected, too. My rules about healthy food had reached an unhealthy point. If I couldn't find something "healthy" to eat, I would just go without food. The "pushing, stress, overworking, high performance, get sick" cycle was starting to become a nasty pattern. Why couldn't a good girl also be wildly successful? Maybe if I tried harder and got creative with the rules, I'd work out the magic formula.

Looking back at my childhood and early school years, the signs were there pretty early. I was a happy, creative child, but I always wanted to know all the answers, win the game, make everyone like me. Strongly empathetic, I was easily affected by the news and the horrors of the world.

I remember having nightmares about the Hiroshima bombings we learned about in school, the whales being hunted, the rainforest being destroyed. I was vegetarian on and off throughout school. I wanted to save all the animals, join Greenpeace, save the world.

I developed my first stress-related condition at age twelve. As a young child, I noticed that people listened to actors who spoke about environmental issues. If I could become an actor, I could really help the world to be a better place.

I declared my intentions to my parents and got started. Thankfully, theatre was a fantastic creative outlet for me. I had lots of theatre friends who understood my stress and my silly side. Keeping in mind I wanted to make this my career, I was regularly involved with multiple productions. My parents were supportive of my dreams but cautioned that I needed to have a backup career, because actors were so often unemployed. I took that advice to heart and made getting straight "As" about maximizing my choices. Maybe if I wasn't an actor, I could be a scientist or a doctor.

I was internally driven, but external approval became more and more important. Perfectionism can be like that. There are many perceived good and bad elements. Often, the achievements are encouraged, but the obsession and anxiety are overlooked. The pressure to get the next high grade, or get the next role in a play, robbed the enjoyment. I used to joke that I was a type-A personality trying to be a type-B!

When your head is this busy and noisy, you are often quite disconnected from what you need and want. It becomes hard to feel centered with a storm around you! I longed for holidays, weekends, and time away; this is always a sign that you're not enjoying your daily life. When getting away is a survival need, rather than a pleasure, something has to shift.

I learned to start resting and to build self-care into my schedule. I created strategies so I could keep performing, keep "managing," and keep getting those grades. Self-care can easily become one more thing you're not doing and another way to feel bad about yourself. I tried to relax after my massage, to spend time reading for pleasure, to go out dancing with my girlfriends just for the fun of it.

My breaking point really came when I was running my

business, teaching for a natural health college, and had recently finished working on a research team for a high profile natural health study. I was also engaged, living in a lovely house in a good neighbourhood, and we had a puppy.

My external measures of success were rating extremely high—I was in love, had great friends and family, and I was using many aspects of my education and training. I was also exhausted!

I remember the day I realized something was really wrong. I had been running an exam for my class, and in the quiet, I found I had a little time to start thinking about why I felt so tired. I was doing too much, stressed again, and I was on day 19 of a really long period.

I went to the doctor, and after some uncomfortable tests, I found out I had polycystic ovarian syndrome and thyroid issues. Years later, I came to realize the extent of my adrenal exhaustion and that it had been there for years. Of course, all of these things are connected and take time to unravel.

Then came the years of seeking—seeking help, seeking treatment, and seeking healing protocols. I tried many things. They all helped to varying degrees.

After my wedding, I went back to uni to study nutrition. Sadly, the academic perfectionism reared its ugly head again, and despite realizing that being up at 1:00 a.m. finishing assignments wasn't improving my health, I couldn't seem to unhook.

This time, I didn't feel my self-esteem was wrapped up in it, but I wanted those high marks badly. For the most part, I was a lot more balanced in my approach, although I kept my business going and increased my teaching load. I achieved my academic goals and was top of my year level, but my passion wasn't being met.

This was when I switched to holistic nutrition and health coaching. More personal development and study became an adventure, and I had people with me along for the ride. I got to help others, and I got learn, laugh, and discover more about myself and what really worked for me and my clients.

We're all different, and that's part of what is so beautiful about this journey; it shifts and changes as we do.

The sneaky thing is that most people are stressed, and so it starts to feel normal—but competitive stress is a game where everybody loses! Friends catch up, and the stress pours out; we discuss what's wrong and how hard things are, and sometimes it helps. Sometimes we vent and connect, support and strategize, laugh, cry, and see the positives.

Unfortunately, when we're caught in a stress cycle, it's all too easy to play comparisons, pick up each other's stress, and even escalate it. What you focus on expands—this fits both the Universal Law perspective and neurophysiology.

Our brain looks for more of what we focus on and filters the incredible amount of information coming in to fit our perspective and focus. When we're feeling stressed and overwhelmed, we see more stressors and get even more overwhelmed. The awesome thing about this is that by shifting our perspective and focus, we experience a different world, (or at least have a different experience of the world). We get to choose!

Sometimes, the way to deal with stress isn't to make it

wrong or to wait until you break down to have your breakthrough; it's to redefine your version of success. What does having it all even mean? It's pretty unlikely that fitting into someone else's boxes will tick all of yours. We don't have enough time or energy to "do it all" on someone else's terms, so what if we did what was important, what was fun, what works for us? And what if we enjoyed the journey to finding out?

When you rest and look after yourself in the way that nourishes and nurtures YOU, you have more energy and more resources—not just so you can keep giving and working, but so you get to enjoy your life! Bring on the self-care, the fun, and the relaxed, unstructured time with loved ones and yourself!

Kylie Firns

Kylie believes that we are all capable of amazing things.

Discovering Pilates after a serious back injury during military service, Kylie later founded Pilates Ballarat to offer a uniquely customised experience of the Pilates method, gymnastics-based strength, and mobility fundamentals.

Kylie's entrepreneurialism and ambition are driven by the precepts that opportunities are disguised as hard work and that without great risk there is no great reward.

A passionate food enthusiast, her creativity extends to the kitchen where she enjoys the challenge of making nutritious and great tasting food.

She enjoys spending time with her husband, son, and puppy.

www.pilatesballarat.com.au
kylie.firns@gmail.com

COMPILED by **KRISTY-LEA TRITZ**

Chapter 22

THE LITTLE GIRL WHO COULD

Kylie Firns

I never felt loved as a child. My parents broke each other's hearts; when they looked at me, all they saw were painful memories. I was a reminder of how much they hated each other. I become a chameleon and learned to blend into my surroundings.

I was taught to ignore the real me. I survived, in a war zone of neglect, fear, violence, and hatred. The loneliness throughout my life fuelled me, filled up my tank, and turned me into the little girl who could!

I wasn't aware I have superpowers, but I do! I have the incredible ability of finding people who are good, kind, and who love and believe in me.

Age ten, enter Mrs. M and Mr. L, who lived around the corner from me. Their adorable child, B, became my "adoptive" sibling. I don't remember how I met them, but they took me in, kept me safe, and loved me. Being loved was the strangest feeling. So very addictive. I always needed more. A kind word or a warm cuddle was never ever enough. I was hooked on this chemical reaction. I'd give anything to have it.

In my early teens, I went years without this feeling. It was horrendous! I had zero friends. My family stood by, watching me get beat up by my father. It was then I wanted to take my own life for the first time.

I remember one afternoon in particular, I wanted to die. I had been suspended from school. The thought that my father had been called was my worst nightmare. I rode my bike as far away as my legs could take me. I was numb. I did not want to be on this earth anymore. I quit.

Or so I thought. The weirdest thing is, I didn't get a beating for this event; I got grounded. Yep, grounded!

The second time I recognized my favourite stimulant, LOVE, was during my mid-teens. For the first time in my life, I made friends at school. I felt a sense of belonging and acceptance. A few of my friends' mums took me in and offered a maternal kindness. My first real hit of exclusive love came from N. I was delirious. His parents abundantly loved me, too. I thought I might overdose! Living in fear at home didn't matter, I was learning the true power of love.

Family life got worse. I realized after spending time with the adults raising me—my mother and stepfather, my father, and stepmother—that I did not belong. They were not good people, and that's being polite. They constantly attacked me —an innocent and trusting child. They were horrible to the people around them, even the ones they "loved." They became quintessential examples of who not to be.

I ran away from my father at sixteen. Homeless, really, I was depressed and extremely destructive. I smoked pot just to feel numb. I liked the smile that being high put across my face, almost like I was happy. I had no idea what happy was, though, as I was still deep into survival mode.

My self-destructive behaviour continued. I tried to fulfill

my promise of being the exact opposite of my family. I found that opposition through volunteering. I worked for various charities, any organization that could keep me occupied and away from home.

Along with the distraction, I got to see how small things like helping another person made them feel that sense of love that I ached for. Giving felt just as good as receiving. I was called good things: smart, kind, helpful, considerate, hard-working. They never called me dumb, stupid, a waste of space, dirty, deceitful, lazy, unlovable. Maybe, just maybe, these people were right. A very long battle began in my head.

Post-traumatic stress disorder was the diagnosis at age thirty-one. Finally! A label for the battle I was going through. After constantly being told that it was all in my head, having a professional acknowledge that I was abused was hard to accept.

I was advised by others in my life to forgive my wrong-doers. What a load of shit! No one who hurt me in my family has acknowledged my hurt, let alone been sorry for the fact —how could they deserve forgiveness? I choose a different kind of forgiveness: "Forgiveness is giving up the hope that the past could be different, it's accepting the past for what it was, using this moment and this time to help yourself move forward." Thank you, Oprah Winfrey, you got it right.

Before joining the military, I lived with my mother, stepfather and two of my half-siblings. It felt decent, almost. But I was never able to be me. I knew my mother would never physically hurt me, as she was a coward. But she used her words like knives, always aimed at my heart. As for my father, our relationship was distant and cold. The first time in my life he was even slightly respectful of me was when my mother and I attacked him financially. For my father, money was the only motivator.

I tried so hard to get my mother to like me. I even asked her to be my friend. Her reply still cuts me deeper than all the physical abuse I went through: "I would never have you as a friend. I don't like you."

My own mother did not like me! At a basic level, she despised me, and it was obvious. As I left her house to pursue a stint in the army, there she was, saying her goodbyes with my siblings at her sides. I still have no idea why a psychopath does what they do but with such confidence she said, "This is what happens when you love someone, J; they leave you." My darling siblings had a look of pure sadness, like I'd shown and felt many times throughout my childhood.

I don't have any regrets, but I do feel pain when it comes to my siblings. I love them dearly and would love to have a connection with them. They don't know me, have a relationship with me, or even get the choice to do so. It saddens me it's this way.

Kids do not know violence, they learn it. Like I did. I still fight the urge to be like my parents. The choice is worth the work. You can always choose to be who you want to be; you may make mistakes, but you choose at the start of every day who you want to be and the impact you want to make.

I joined the army at eighteen. Somewhat ironically, it was a decision of self-preservation. I no longer felt welcome in my mother's house either. There was no proof that any part of my family loved or wanted me. The military was a fabulous step up in my life. Training was tough, mentally and physically. Despite injury and a lack of self-worth, I graduated.

The military provided both high highs and low lows. On one hand, I had found a sense of camaraderie, and on the other, I was forced to endure bullying. I accepted an opportunity for a special circumstance posting to a different location where I would eventually meet my husband and find my heart in Pilates.

I am a free thinker! Military service was my catalyst for self-belief and personal growth. Hard work and difficult times became opportunities for reevaluation and growth. In my experience, the tougher the situation, the greater the reward. Stick to your guns and see the bad times through; good things will come if you want them to.

I've been kicked and pulled down by every single person in my life that was in a position of authority. I considered giving up too many times to count. The battle of "What if they are right? I am worthless and shouldn't have been born" versus "I am a great person and really making a difference" was my toughest fight of all. With lots of work, and lots of good loving people, I can now say that I won. Not them. Not the haters.

They helped me get to where I am today. Without all my hardships, I would not be here. I now know I am kind, loving, considerate, hardworking, driven, strong, willful, patient, and all the good things I hoped to be. I am all of those things, because I used my experiences to learn these skills. I am a butterfly, flapping my wings and sharing my beauty with the world.

COMPILED by **KRISTY-LEA TRITZ**

Laura Probert

Laura Probert, MPT, has practiced physical therapy over twenty years. She is the owner of Bodyworks Physical Therapy and the author of *Warrior Love: A Journal to Inspire Your Fiercely Alive Whole Self* and *Living, Healing, and Taekwondo.* Through her brand of physical therapy, her writing, and the martial arts, she hopes to inspire people to find their own inner warrior. Laura also hosts a writing group on Facebook called When Your Soul Speaks.

www.bewarriorlove.com
www.bodyworksptonline.com
bodyworspt@comcast.net
facebook.com/laura.probert.3 & /warriorlove
twitter.com/livehealTKD

COMPILED by **KRISTY-LEA TRITZ**

Chapter 23

FEAR: MY GREATEST TEACHER

Laura Probert

I believe that every situation in life can be your teacher. My greatest teacher so far has been fear, for fear has revealed the path to passion, joy, and love. It has provided the freedom to live my deepest desires and left me feeling fiercely alive.

Living my life in fear has kept me small and helpless. The people and situations in my life that trigger that fear usually do it by making me feel like I have done something bad or wrong. Feeling scolded, I actually become that small, helpless, fearful child, powerless in the old conditioned beliefs.

When someone is upset with me, critical of something I have done, or in disagreement with my thoughts, words, or actions, I crumble, turning into that quiet, ashamed little girl. I am powerless in those moments, with a deep ache in my heart and a tight clench in my gut. The fear of punishment sits inside of me, eating away at my spirit. I sit still and silent, trying not to be noticed, trying to be a good girl.

Living this way has affected every relationship I have ever had with a man, including my current spouse—even many relationships with women friends. It renders me voiceless, avoiding confrontation at all cost, afraid to express my truest self for fear it isn't good or worthy.

At some point in my childhood, I learned that what I thought and felt was wrong. The problem with this is that the people closest to me haven't gotten to know the real me. After eighteen years of marriage, I am finally starting to speak up, and I am not totally sure my husband knows what to make of it.

Awareness of the fear voice in my head became a key to healing the deepest, ugliest, most shameful parts of my soul. The parts that have kept me feeling small, unworthy, and not enough, and the ones that have kept me quiet. I learned to recognize the voice.

Today, every time I hear that familiar voice, I smile, knowing I am being given another opportunity to go deeper and learn more from this teacher. I know the treasures waiting for me in those lessons. My greatest fears have ended up my biggest triumphs.

In 2012, I wrote and self-published my first book, an inspirational memoir about my life and healing journey through the martial art of Tae Kwon Do. This was the beginning of speaking my truth, using my voice, and sharing myself with others—including my own husband.

I was about to realize one of my biggest dreams, and I was terrified. The voice inside reminded me I was a nobody, that I wasn't good enough, that nobody cared about my story, and that writing it was a waste of time, or worse, could get me into trouble.

I questioned everything. Maybe I should have written something different, or less personal, or more helpful. Doubt and judgment flooded my mind. I had shared some of my most vulnerable self on pages for the world to see, and I was still afraid to be me and cared way too much about whether others liked me and my story.

Trying to live up to a lifetime of good girl training, I was desperately afraid of failure, even in my successes. I couldn't separate from the fear, and it continued to paralyze me, keeping my passion and joy locked up inside.

In Tae kwon Do, when you earn your black belt and you think you know everything, your teacher will remind you that it is just the beginning of your journey. Writing my story, I came to realize, was just the beginning of my journey with healing fear. I was becoming a warrior but still had a lot of training to do.

To transform my relationship with fear, I had to face it, whether it was confronting an employee, competing in a tournament, or standing up for what I believed in in my own marriage.

Tae kwon Do has been a steadfast teacher, consistently placing me in fear's path, giving me ample opportunities to practice. This martial art became a way of life. :"You must do the thing you think you cannot do." And this one by my master John L. Holloway: "Discipline the mind—the body will follow."

Another healing art, called John F. Barnes Myofascial Release, also catapulted me into the middle of the arena, where fear waited like a crouching tiger. It has given me tools, like the shield and the sword, but most profoundly, the language of the tiger herself.

I can now communicate with fear, "I see you, I hear you, thank you for trying to protect me, but I got this." When fear tries to get inside, shut me down, and keep me from feeling, I recognize it, and that simple awareness disarms her. With awareness and courage, I take my warrior into the arena and speak tiger.

Being present to my surroundings, and especially to the way I feel inside, allows me to recognize fear as my teacher. I feel the triggers, recognize the opportunities in them, and with this awareness, have a choice how to respond. This allows me to do life from a place of curiosity and courage.

I feel excitement, joy, and passion now more than I ever have in my life. When I am triggered with a remark or criticism, and feel the old feeling of the grip around my heart, I am able to let go sooner and regain my power before I ache. Recognizing my greatest teacher has been a blessing. It has meant freedom, and for that I am grateful.

Grateful for fear? Most would do without it and settle for a life that is easier, less risky, and less raw. Most numb the feelings with drugs, alcohol, overwork, or excessive exercise. If you are numb, you won't feel the fear, but you also won't get to feel the passionate joy that is one of the treasures of the warrior.

When you are afraid, take a moment to feel it, awareness is the key. Step back, make some space, and listen to the voice as an observer. Give your fear a name. Recognize that she is not you. Learn her language. There are many reasons she might be there, many ways she has become a part of your life and beliefs, many dreams she has squelched. But only because you believed her old, outdated, unhelpful messages. Call her out, be awake to her message. Realize your bigger dreams, that allowing her to keep you from them isn't serving the higher meaning and purpose you have come to know for your life.

Recognizing the fear, feeling it fully, and then transforming it into love is how you will do the thing you think you cannot do. I call this warrior love. It is the kind that will change the world.

Be aware. Be you. Be brave. Be a warrior. You are ready to learn the lesson your greatest teacher has offered you, to live your passions and dreams.

The Centre of the Ring

Laura Probert

I am gonna wake up

To the stuff of my life

I won't play small

I'm gonna do it right.

I'll feel what it's like

In the center of the ring

Get my ass kicked

And show up again.

Cuz it's no real fun

To watch from the crowd

Wishing I was there

Shouting out loud to the world.

I am gonna play big

Hear my roar

I will shine out my light

And give a little more.

I'll save seats for those

Who aren't ready to play

Realize their fear

Gets in their way.

I will walk to the center

Of that great big arena

Feel what it's like

To really be seen.

I'll fight my best fight

Speak my full truth

Write my deep thoughts

And connect with you.

Because when I play large

I win the prize

A life full and rich

Among the bright stars.

The best part is when

You catch my starlight

Meet me in the center

Help me to fight.

Alongside each other

We shine so much brighter

What we had alone

Multiplies infinitely together.

A powerful force

Of Warrior Love

Now let's build our team

From those seats above.

Wave to your friends

And critics alike

They all want to play

They all want to fight.

Help them wake up

Help them play large

Help them show up

Even when it's hard.

If they can't take the heat

And you are alone

Show up again

Show them how it's done.

I want to play

I rather stand tall

I will play large

Even if I fall.

Because if there is one thing

I have learned to trust

Being seen, playing big

For me is a must.

The center of the ring

Waits for the warrior

Come, take my hand

We'll kick some ass together

COMPILED by **KRISTY-LEA TRITZ**

Lauren King

After struggling and overcoming her own health issues, Lauren King's mission is to empower as many women as she can to be their healthiest and happiest. She is a successful wellness and weight loss coach and personal trainer.

Lauren runs online coaching programs that help clients adopt a healthier lifestyle and uses the latest breakthrough health products to support her clients' journeys to health. She is also helping other women build their own fulfilling and financially rewarding businesses.

When not working, she is most likely exercising and spending quality time with her loving husband, Ian, and her cherished family.

www.beslimweightloss.com
info@beslimweightloss.com
facebook.com/laurenking#
au.linkedin.com/in/laurenking

Chapter 24

IS THIS AS GOOD AS IT GETS? NO IT GETS BETTER!

Lauren King

I grew up in a loving family in suburban Australia. For the most part, my life was ordinary. Being an only child never affected me. I was surrounded constantly by my cousins and family, so I was never short of company or a feeling of love and family connection.

From the outside looking in, my life was idyllic, but I found it incredibly challenging watching my father continually abuse his body with excessive alcohol and smoking. His health suffered greatly and impacted the whole family. From an early age, I realized that I would never want to take the same path of destruction.

Both of my parents got cancer at a relatively young age, and this was an extremely challenging and very emotional time for us all. The impact it had on me was one of terror, for the possibility maybe losing both my dearest parents horrified me.

At sixty-two, my father died a terrible death from throat and lip cancer. The effects of the cancer were horrible, and he experienced so much pain.

That same year my father died, my marriage to my childhood sweetheart ended. I found myself a single parent of three children. I was in unfamiliar territory, and my life changed dramatically in a short time. I felt as though the life had drained out of every part of my body, and I was just running on auto pilot.

Watching my mother struggle with breast cancer was heartbreaking, because knowing her fear of living with this disease and coping with the side effects of the treatment was such a roller coaster. It was so exhausting for us all.

My mother was known as a glamour girl. One of the cancer drugs she took caused rapid weight gain. She hated being overweight and it caused her to be depressed. My outgoing and lively mother withdrew into herself, hating her body, and being so sick. It deeply saddened me to see her like this.

Unfortunately, my lovely mother eventually lost her battle with cancer. Her death affected me in a way that words cannot express. She was the heart of our family. I felt broken inside knowing that I would never see her again. Never see her smile, nor hear her voice.

After my mother's death, I gained twenty-two pounds. I couldn't lose it no matter what I did. I suffered intolerable pain. I was totally exhausted. Every muscle in my body ached. I spent four days out of the week laid up in bed with terrible headaches and body pain.

I went to all sorts of doctors. Appointment after appointment. No one knew what was wrong with me. I felt like no one was taking me seriously. When I was crying out for help, going through my darkest times, one doctor said to me, "Oh most women get fat at fifty. Just accept the issues that go with it." They thought it was my age, or else it was all in my head. Either way, I wasn't going to accept that diagnosis! Not me, I said to myself with determination. I was not prepared to sit back and accept this. No woman should.

Eventually, I was diagnosed with fibromyalgia, adrenal depletion, underactive thyroid, and chronic fatigue.

After much soul searching, I came to realize that all this physical pain was connected to internal emotions. Suppressed and locked in my subconscious was the trauma and stress from my past: the loss of both my parents; watching their extremely painful deaths; the breakdown of my relationship with my husband; becoming a single parent.

The stories of my past were written in my body. My negative thoughts and feelings had become the physical equivalent. All I could find was temporary relief. I was doing what most people do—focusing on the symptoms instead of getting to the heart of the matter.

I had such a strong belief that there would be an answer. I went to all sorts of practitioners. I tried every supplement and remedy I could get my hands on. You name it, I tried it. I was so obsessed with finding someone or something to heal myself.

I wanted to start living life again instead of just surviving it. I was passionate about living a healthy lifestyle, incorporating whole natural foods, and exercising when I could. I soldiered on even though most days it nearly killed me.

I realized my parents' health struggles impacted me greatly. My fear of the same thing happening to me made wellness a priority in my life. I made a promise to myself, and my dear mother, that I would always take care of my body, mind, and spirit to the best of my ability. This became my passion. I had a huge desire to learn all I could with health, nutrition, fitness, and holistic wellness.

I trained as a personal trainer and became a qualified weight loss consultant. I educated myself on organic natural foods and how powerful they were for healing. I studied weight loss, self-healing, and personal development from a holistic point of view.

After eleven years of this battle, I developed enough knowledge and experience to understand how to look after my body and my emotions enough to minimize my symptoms. I was still suffering a lot of pain.

The healthier I become in mind, body, and spirit, the more my body rejects anything that does me no good. I tune into my feelings and really honour myself. I am much better at self-care and compassion. I know I have to take care of myself, physically and emotionally, at all times. If I don't, my health would be compromised.

I feel extremely blessed and grateful for all I have, for my journey and all the experiences along the way, good and bad. The challenges that I faced have been difficult, but they have also enriched my life, inspiring me to help other women change their lives to become healthier and happier.

The most important thing I learned from all of this is that we have to love and appreciate ourselves. Be kind to ourselves. Feel happy in our own skin. We need to, as women, be confident, have extreme self-worth, and a sense of gratitude for all that we have and are.

Having gained the knowledge and gone through the life

experiences I did, I've gained the skills and tools to help support and guide others who feel lost, at a complete point of despair in their lives. Maybe you even feel that this is as good as gets, but you do not have to accept this! You can choose differently. I know because I did.

I realized life is not one size fits all. But using strategies that are positive, supporting, and motivating gives me and others the answers, power, and belief that there is not only hope but a solution to actually eradicating health issues. They can lead to a healthy happy lifestyle—mind, body, and spirit.

After years of being told from different doctors the same supposed scenario that didn't work and seeing others struggle with their health, my mission became to provide different program options for women who deal with health issues like I did. I wanted to create that change in their lives, to let them know that they were not alone on this journey, and to give them a truly personalized program tailored to their needs, not a medically cookie cutter approach with no result at the end. I had suffered through that cookie cutter approach and knew there was a better way. I knew in order to create and manifest your desires, you needed to be able to truly see, feel, believe, and be willing to trust and allow the body's own process to take place.

There is nothing more rewarding than helping someone come to the complete realization that this doesn't have to be as good as it gets! Through my own battles and having to endure years of struggle and no one truly hearing or believing my situation made me more determined and allowed me to create something life-changing.

COMPILED by **KRISTY-LEA TRITZ**

Lisa McAdams

Lisa McAdams is a speaker, author, life coach, and personal trainer. Lisa is an inspiration to all those that hear her personal story of overcoming incredible challenges to not only survive, but to thrive.

Lisa runs a successful life coaching and personal training business in Sydney, Australia. She speaks regularly at events to inspire other women to live a life that they love, rather than just surviving.

Lisa's signature program, Reclaim Your Life Now, is where she works with recently divorced women struggling with their new identity as a single mum. She helps them navigate their new place in society and with their family and friends and find the confidence to create new life for themselves that both they and their children are proud of.

www.lisamcadams.com
info@lisamcadams.com
facebook.com/lisa.mcadams.963
twitter.com/lisamcadams456

COMPILED by **KRISTY-LEA TRITZ**

Chapter 25

IT STARTS WITH TRUST

Lisa McAdams

As I sat there on the ground, blood flowing from me like a river, it was hard to believe that just moments ago I thought the worst was behind me. Only the night before, I had written a list with my two closest friends of everything I had been through that year alone—this was to lift my spirits from the depression that was taking over. I had even said I would love to spend some time sitting, drinking a latte, with views of Sydney Harbour so I could appreciate all that I had achieved.

I had escaped England and a childhood of abuse, and now I had finally escaped domestic violence and was safe. I had escaped from my violent husband three months before for the sixth time. Only this time, I had done it right. I went to a shelter for women and children suffering from domestic violence, took proper advice, and went to court to get an interim apprehended violence order (AVO).

Just ten days prior to this accident, I was transferred to a safe house. My friend came to lunch with her two children to see my new home and celebrate the fact my son, my daughter, and I were finally safe. I was standing on the table trying to put in the umbrella of my patio table and that's when it happened—the glass cracked and I was pulled through, headfirst. Now, here I sat in my own blood.

I felt strangely calm; in fact, I had never been so calm. Time was passing slowly. I was aware of every micro second. All I could concentrate on was keeping my son, who was only two, away from me. I had blood pouring down the right side of my face that I didn't want him to see. I was unsure if my face was damaged or where the blood was coming from. What I did know is that I was surrounded by broken glass and my son's feet were bare. I was giving my friend instructions. Put the babies in the cot. Call the ambulance. I was in total control. I sat there for what seemed like an eternity, listening to the sound of my own blood pouring down the drain.

I didn't really react until I was in the ambulance and I knew my children were safely indoors. What gripped me, though, wasn't pain or thoughts of my own life but an overwhelming feeling of my children being alone in this world without me to protect them. I was all they had. Did anyone really understand just how dangerous their dad was?

When I arrived at the ER, I told everybody who would listen that I had an interim violence order in place and not to call their father. The thought of him getting them hurt far more than the thick shards of glass that were embedded in me from head to toe. My situation seemed impossible. How could life be so cruel after all that I had endured? Why me? Why now? My belief in the good in this world had gone. I was broken.

I was telling myself, "I give up. This is too much to bear," when a voice from somewhere deep inside of me said, "Just trust me." Trust? I had never had anyone to trust in my life. I didn't even know how. I wanted evidence. I wanted facts.

Inside my head, I screamed, "Give me a reason, any reason to trust!" But all I got back was, "Just trust me." Then it occurred to me I had nothing left to lose. If I could trust, my children had a lot to gain. I decided right there and then, on that gurney waiting to go into surgery, that I would trust and that I would trust with my whole heart.

After surgery, I was taken to the serious burns unit, the one unit in any hospital that they can lock down in a second if there is a risk of infection spreading to the burn patients. I was there because of the risk of my husband finding me. I felt relatively safe but worried for my children.

My friends had bought me in some latte sachets, and after three days in bed, the nurse told me I needed to get up and sit in the chair because she was worried about my state of mind. She kindly made me a latte and helped me to a chair in my room. As she opened the blinds, I saw the most beautiful view of Sydney, just as I had requested. Far from the circumstances I had imagined, but there all the same.

I took this as a sign that I was right to trust. I now believed to the core of my being that I was in charge of my destiny, that if I kept believing in myself, I could build myself a good life.

This new belief was tested later that same day. I was in my hospital room with my friend, my children, a social worker, and a physiotherapist there for my first session. My friend's phone rang; as she listened, she went white and left the room. Before she returned, she called the social worker into the hallway. As I watched them talk, I knew this was bad. Fear gripped every fibre of my body.

As they returned to my room, my worst fears were

realized. I was right; my husband did indeed know where I was. He had just happily told my friend's husband, knowing they would have to tell me. I had trusted somebody that I now knew I shouldn't have trusted.

I knew right then and there that I needed to leave the hospital and I needed to leave right away. The hospital staff tried to convince me to stay, but my children were only covered in the violence order if they were with me. As they weren't allowed to stay in the hospital with me, I would have to leave with them.

A fast and farcical departure from the hospital ensued. I was nowhere near ready to leave. I could still not bear weight on my right leg.

The next few weeks were challenging beyond my imagining. My friends would come in every night to help my children and I get ready for bed, make dinner, and clean up. To this day, I don't know how I would have coped without them. This was the first lesson from my accident—I learned to trust people not because I wanted to but because I had to.

My rehabilitation was to be as long as it was painful. I was nearly thirty-nine. Ever since I was a teenager, I had dreamed of running a marathon when I was forty. I still believed this dream was possible, even though I was now struggling to walk. When I told to my doctor, I could see she found it amusing that I still thought this was a possibility. She told me to be realistic and concentrate on the hope that one day I would be able to walk without the pain taking my leg from under me.

What the doctor didn't know was that I had trust and the

belief that I could do anything I set my heart on. Just twenty months later, in my fortieth year, I ran the Sydney Marathon in an impressive four hours and twenty minutes. I was still in pain, and I always will be. I was later diagnosed with something called neuropathic pain in my right leg. My brain, due to the extreme stress when my accident happened, had not registered that I was better and was still continuously sending pain signals.

The pain doesn't stop me from doing the things I love, but it took five years for me to manage the pain enough to run my next marathon. Last year, I ran the New York City Marathon. I had glandular fever this past year, and it really knocked my health around, but I'm not letting that stand in my way. I am training for the 2015 London Marathon and writing a book about the experience.

The neuropathic pain is something I still manage on a daily basis. But this pain, like the child abuse, domestic violence, and the subsequent mental health challenges I had to overcome—it will not win. I continue to believe anything is possible if I can dream it, turn it into a goal, make a plan, and take action every single day to make that dream a reality. It all started with trust and the decision to believe in the dream. I mean really believe.

I read this when I was very young, and it is how I have and always will live my life:

"Someone said it couldn't be done, but I, with a chuckle, replied, 'Maybe it couldn't, but I would be one who never said no 'til I tried.'"

COMPILED by **KRISTY-LEA TRITZ**

Rebecca Thompson

Rebecca Thompson was born and raised in Saskatchewan. Upon graduation from high school, she attended Briercrest College and Seminary where she earned a Master of Arts degree in Marriage and Family Counselling. Rebecca currently resides in Edmonton, Alberta and has worked with high risk youth throughout her career. She has spent nearly the last decade as an Addictions Counsellor for youth and their families. Rebecca is married to a wonderful man named Scott and together they have a son named Liam on Earth and a son named Xavier in Heaven. Xavier is the inspiration for this chapter and this is part of his legacy.

thesethreeremain@gettotheheartofthematter.ca

facebook.com/thesethreeremain

twitter.com/these_3_remain

COMPILED by **KRISTY-LEA TRITZ**

Chapter 26

THESE THREE REMAIN: LIFE AFTER LOSING XAVIER

Rebecca Thompson

On December 14, 2013, we found out that I was pregnant with our second child and were ecstatic. We always wanted our son, who is now two, to have a little brother or sister. I felt so excited knowing that next Christmas we would be a family of four. It was initially our little secret, kept between the three of us.

It had been a dream of mine since I was fifteen years old to travel to Jamaica and that dream became a reality in February 2014. While at a waterfall called Dunn's River Falls, I was taking a photograph of my husband and son when I started to feel blood trickle down my leg. I began to scream! Climbing down the stairs to the first-aid shack, I yelled at tourists to please pray for my baby. Emergency staff placed me on a stretcher. I was whisked across the beach with the sun down blazing upon me, and was placed in an ambulance. I prayed that our baby would be okay. I recall my son lifting up my shirt, placing his hands on me, closing his eyes, and laying his face on my belly. My husband and I knew that we were witnessing a very surreal and spiritual moment, as we believe that he knew what was going on. I was then taken to a hospital in the town of St. Ann's Bay, where staff and patients boldly prayed for me and my baby. The ultrasound revealed that everything was fine. Relief swept over me.

Shortly after arriving back home in Canada, my husband and I were watching a movie. I got up from my chair to fetch us a snack, and found myself in a pool of blood. My husband called 9-1-1 and I was taken to our local hospital. This was the first of many trips there as the bleeding continued for the next couple of months. I was diagnosed with a subchorionic hemorrhage and was placed on bed rest indefinitely. I lived in constant fear. There were times when I would put my hand down the toilet to make sure that I hadn't lost my precious baby, as the clots that I was shedding were so large.

On April 3, 2014, I went to the washroom and discovered that my baby's umbilical cord was out. My friend, who I had been talking on the phone with, called my husband at his work and notified him of what was happening. I called 9-1-1 and waited at the bottom of my stairs for Emergency Medical Services to arrive. As we left my home, I begged one of the paramedics to bring my camera along as I thought that I might need it to photograph my baby. While lying on the stretcher in the ambulance I began to pray, but words would not come. I knew in my heart that my baby's spirit had left my body.

After arriving at the hospital, my husband met me there with tears in his eyes. The doctor used a fetal doppler to check for our baby's heartbeat and we heard one! My hopes were raised, but then she said to me, "That heartbeat is your own." Since we were in a Catholic hospital, they sent me for one final ultrasound. The ultrasound technician told us, "I know that you want there to be hope, but I'm sorry, there isn't any." It seemed that our whole world began to cave in.

Our dreams, future plans, and all of our innocence were robbed from us in a single second.

We were placed in a special room where miscarried and stillborn babies are delivered. I was relieved that I wouldn't have to be in the regular labour and delivery rooms listening to the moans of women in labour and the cries of the babies being born alive. The nurses were so kind and gentle and assured us that our baby was in Heaven. Shortly after being given labour induction medication, I experienced the most excruciating physical pain imaginable. The anesthesiologist and nurses gave me an epidural and laughing gas, but nothing seemed to bring relief. I remember the room being so black and yelling for my husband. I felt that I was living a real life nightmare. There was nothing worse than going through labour, knowing that there wasn't a new life at the end of the suffering.

On April 4, 2014, at 5:31 a.m., I delivered our second son, Xavier Grey Thompson. He was 19 ½ weeks old. I eagerly held my sweet baby boy in my arms. He was so tiny, weighing only 220 grams. He had my husband's bushy blonde eyebrows, my large head, and a cleft lip. The nurses took Xavier's handprints and footprints, as well as several photos of him. These items have since become our treasured keepsakes. Xavier's big brother was brought to the hospital to meet him. Our hospital chaplain and our own pastors were the only other people who got to meet Xavier as we had a special naming ceremony for him. We named him after a superhero and a saint, which seemed appropriate. It was extremely difficult for me to leave the hospital with empty arms.

After leaving the hospital, I thought about how I had

wanted to tell Xavier that I loved him, and was worried that I hadn't. My husband assured me that I had told him this a million times, but I didn't remember. I wanted to see him again, but I wasn't sure if I would be able to, as we had agreed to have an autopsy completed as per our doctor's advice. We would find out weeks later that Xavier had died due to placental abruption, as a result of the subchorionic hemorrhage. However, a couple of days later we were able to go to the hospital to see him for the last time. The hospital staff had dressed him so beautifully; he really looked like a little angel. Professional photographs of Xavier and our family were taken, thanks to our dear friend. This was our final opportunity to see him, kiss him, and tell him how much we loved him.

The hardest moment of my life was closing the little casket and walking away, never to see my baby again. A little wooden urn with a teddy bear engraved on it was chosen to contain his ashes. There was deep meaning behind the teddy bear for me. For Xavier's first birthday I had planned to throw him a teddy bear picnic themed party, and had already started purchasing decorations. After praying with our chaplain, I felt led to host a teddy bear picnic themed memorial. We held the memorial in our backyard, and over a hundred people attended. We collected teddy bears for other baby loss families, as well as money for the Mercy Ships cleft lip and palate surgery programs. I recall my pastor wrapping his arm around me and saying, "Your son has made more of an impact in his short life than some people make in their entire lives."

I have learned so much since losing Xavier. His short life changed mine. His life mattered and he made a difference. Throughout this grief journey I have found myself learning more about God, myself, and my relationships with others. Xavier has given me and my family several gifts. 1 Corinthians 13:13 states, "And now these three remain: faith, hope and love. But the greatest of these is love."

Faith is the first gift that Xavier has given me. I find it very difficult to comprehend that my baby's death was part of a divine plan. However, I take comfort in knowing that Xavier never had to be exposed to the pain and cruelty of this world. All he ever knew was love, as he went directly from my love into Jesus' love. I am learning to trust God even when I don't understand His plans.

Hope is another gift that Xavier has given me. I have a greater hope for eternal life after experiencing the tragic loss of my baby. After losing Xavier God gave me a vision of him playing with birds in Heaven. I really look forward to the day when we will be reunited for all eternity. Hope is what makes my life worth living.

Love is truly the greatest gift that Xavier has given me. I have grieved deeply because I loved him so much. Losing Xavier has helped me to grow in love for God, my husband, my son, and others who are grieving. I have learned more about showing God's love in practical ways. I have found great comfort when people have said "I'm sorry for your loss", and have said Xavier's name. I have also felt strongly supported when people have listened, given hugs, given sympathy cards or meaningful gifts, brought food, helped clean our house, and provided childcare to our eldest son. By following the examples of others, I am now attempting to model what it means to truly help grieving people.

Not a day goes by that my heart doesn't ache, as I

desperately miss Xavier. I continue to hurt, but at the same time I have experienced God's healing through His Holy Spirit and through the words and deeds of people. I know that God is with me while I walk through the valley of the shadow of death. Though our baby has departed Earth and entered into Heaven, our family of three remains, moving forward with faith, hope, and love.

Samantha Dobler

Samantha Dobler is a wife and full-time mom of one with a second on the way! When she was invited to write for this project, it didn't take much for her to readily agree. She wanted to make sure that she was able to write about something that would mean much more than a few pages in a book. "I really hope this resonates with women across the world." Currently, she spends her weekends hosting birthday parties for little girls and weekdays catering to her growing family.

www.luminamobilekids.blogspot.com
luminalashstudio@gmail.com
facebook.com/luminamobilekids
twitter.com/luminalashstudi

Chapter 27

SURVIVING THE JUNGLE OF POSTPARTUM DEPRESSION

Samantha Dobler

Six weeks? Is this some kind of joke? I experienced postpartum for nearly nine months! It was the worst feeling of self-worth I have ever felt in my life. I pretty much hated myself. I hated my new precious baby, and most of all, I hated my spouse. It didn't matter what he did to "help"—in my mind it wasn't enough.

I took pre-baby arrival classes with a nurse, and I remembered one of the things she said was, "Whatever you do, don't hurt that baby, just put him down in the crib and walk away." Admittedly, that was probably the only thing I actually took away from the two-day seminar.

When we arrived home, after our three-day stay at the hospital, I had this overwhelming feeling that NOTHING was done. The house never felt clean enough. If the chores weren't done, who was going to do them? Certainly not my father-in-law, who was staying with us at the time. Not my husband who was working ten hours or more a day. It was all on me! I couldn't do them. Six weeks post-surgery, and in that time, I was not allowed to carry anything more than the baby. Everything just went downhill.

It started when I couldn't force myself out of bed. I would literally lie like a lioness in bed with my little cub beside me, nursing while I slept. Sleep seemed to be my only escape. I would eat dinner with my husband, breakfast only if I could make it down the stairs, but really other than that I didn't eat.

I never wanted kids.

It was like God blessed me specifically with a sleepy baby. He would sleep between fifteen to twenty hours a day! Huge bonus for me, since I spent almost every hour in bed sleeping. I needed the sleep. I needed the escape. Reality wasn't making very much sense, and I hated every moment of being awake.

The second bonus, of course, was that Alex didn't cry very much. He would stare at me for hours with his gray-blue eyes while I tried cooing to him. Being a new mom did not come naturally to me. It was more like someone handed me a cabbage patch doll and said, "By midnight, it will be alive—good luck!"

I had no clue what to do with him, other than change his diapers and nurse him. I had no "deep connection" that other mothers would talk about. I didn't feel connected. I felt like a sea urchin and a fish—a symbiotic relationship, but we weren't in love.

Then I stopped producing milk. Only eight weeks into this new job and I couldn't perform up to standards. I asked for help from our doctor, who prescribed me pills to help with milk production. After another four weeks, I gained so much weight from them and felt like I was starving all the time, I threw them away and said, "Screw it! He will just have to use formula." I gained around forty pounds in a three-month space. Just wonderful. Size 2 to size 14. EXCELLENT!

My sex life? What sex life? I didn't want my spouse to admire my new big body. And my great new scar tissue from my C-section on my midsection—sexy? No, definitely not. I was kind of lucky, though. I used almond oil on my tummy throughout my pregnancy and post-baby. I didn't add stretch marks to my list of "wrong with me." So for that I was grateful.

At the three-month mark, our house was broken into. I had gotten up early because I heard the baby crying and began my morning routine of making formula. I walked back down the hallway on the main floor and I noticed our front door had damage to it. I don't think I have skipped upstairs so fast and quietly in all my life. I figured they must still be in the house. I was shaking and in tears as I woke up my husband.

I remember that moment, how ferocious he looked, half-naked, grabbing the nearest weapon—a bike wrench—and heading downstairs. I gave the baby his bottle, closed his door, and went back to my room and hid. Yup. Those are motherly instincts right there, right? I guess my thought was that if the baby had his bottle and was quiet, whoever might be in our house wouldn't find him.

While I was on the phone reporting the break-in, I had the baby between my legs looking up at me. He smiled. That was the first time our baby smiled at me. I think a bit of my frozen iceberg melted. It felt like, no matter what I did that day or what happened, it wouldn't matter. This little creature, this parasite, liked me.

Our son learned to walk by eight and half months. Why? I didn't do anything for him. I felt like a gazelle on the African

Plains. If this kid was going to survive, he needed to learn to do things himself—and he did, very quickly.

Christmas was around the corner, and the hustle and bustle made things pretty fun. I do remember ENJOYING the shopping and picking out items for our little guy. I was good at shopping. He was good at being good, so I didn't mind taking him with me.

I remember Christmas morning, specifically. This is when all my walls collapsed. When all the terrible thoughts of giving my son away, of hating my spouse, of hating myself dissolved into nothingness.

I remember this day not because it was joyous, fun, and exciting as most of my Christmases have been. I remember this because of the panic that set in that morning when we could not reach my friend, Michelle. I remember the tears my sister cried when she confirmed what little details she could on the phone. I listened to the deafening confirmation that my dear friend was gone.

Michelle was a very big part of my life. She was more than just a friend to me. She was my ear when I needed someone to listen, my shoulder when I couldn't bear my own thoughts. Michelle was an amazing person, and more than that, she was also a mom.

Michelle left us suddenly. She was involved in a car accident. What I didn't expect was for her baby to survive. Her baby is a month younger than my own son.

That was the day I hugged my son and realized how stupid I had been, how much I LOVED my son. I hugged my husband, too, and realized how in love I was with this person who had helped me, this person who really just wanted the best for me. My little family. That moment in my life when everything fell apart was also the moment in my life when all the puzzle pieces finally fit together.

I never felt like I fit. I never felt like I belonged anywhere. I felt like, when Michelle left her baby behind, it dawned on me that her baby would never really get to meet her mommy. Never get to experience those hugs and kisses. Never get to go to her first day of school while Michelle teared up. I felt like all those experiences that I had just thrown away for the last nine months were completely wasted, because I just didn't understand where I fit in.

Now I know what it means to be a mommy. I know what it means to be truly in love with my son. I know that when we have our second baby, we will have an easier time because I know who I am now. I have never wasted another moment with my son. Every one of those minutes I have spent with my son, I remember now. I treasure. I keep thinking...What if that was me and my son had to grow up without me? I didn't want that.

What can you do when you have postpartum?

J–Just relax! Lower your expectations and "do it later." Trust me, laundry and dishes never cease, so do it as you go and don't make that today's priority.

U–Understand that you are the most important person in your spouse's and child's life. If you need help, reach out to your spouse, a sister, your mother, an aunt, or seek professional help. Doctors are better equipped to handle postpartum now more than ever.

COMPILED by **KRISTY-LEA TRITZ**

N–Never devalue yourself. You are worth so much more than you will ever realize. You are still YOU!

G–Goof off. Don't want to do anything today? Want to take a day off? Want to take a *week* off? Do that—just make sure whatever you choose to do, you are happy and your child is happy.

L–Lie down. Take a nap. One in the afternoon? Nap time. You are allowed to take "mini-breaks"

E–Expect the unexpected and take it with grace. Everything will happen. The best and the worst of all kinds —just let it happen and work your way through it. You really are a superhero. You just don't have to wear the cape every day.

Shannon Riley

Shannon Riley has a passion for helping people. She started her own company in 2014 called Cre8 Change. With Cre8 Change, Shannon is able to help people through her numerous modalities as a bodyworker. She has been trained through the NSPA, the C.H.E.K. Institute, NeuroKinetic Therapy, and most recently, she is in massage school. When she is not helping others with their injuries or movement dysfunctions, she loves traveling and being outdoors with her wife and three pups.

www.cre8change4u.com
www.shanvice.com
shan.riley13@yahoo.com
facebook.com/shannon.riley13
twitter.com/shanriley13

COMPILED by **KRISTY-LEA TRITZ**

Chapter 28

LIFE'S CURVEBALL: SUICIDE'S OTHER SIDE

Shannon Riley

Life has a funny way of throwing curveballs. I had a vision of how I thought my life would go. I was taught by society at a young age that there is an order to life: elementary school, middle school, high school, college, job, house, marriage, babies, grandbabies. It was the blueprint of my life.

I first got to know him my sophomore year of high school. He was an incoming freshman and I was helping the "newbies" out with their lockers. He couldn't open his locker and I saw him struggling so I walked over to help him.

Athletics was our common love. He was truly my "high school sweetheart." He was good-looking, athletic, popular... he had it all. We both had it all. Everything had fallen into place. I know it was high school and we were young, but I was truly happy.

We dated throughout high school and into my freshman year of college. And shared so many firsts together. He was my rock. He was the kind of guy who always made me laugh, who wrote me little sweet notes and was able to make me smile, day in and day out. On the outside, everything was perfect. We shared an amazing high school experience together.

Now when I look back at high school, I just think about how everything went so wrong. It's like someone came and threw a can of black paint over my picture perfect life.

March 12, 2001. It's a date I will never forget. It's where my blueprint got ripped to pieces. The week prior to this was filled with so much confusion. I received a call of concern over him. They told me to come home. I heard he had started on some kind of medication. He was acting out of character, and I knew I had to confront him to find out what the truth was. I had a sense that something was terribly wrong, and that he needed me. I felt angry and confused.

At this point, I had never had my heart broken. I so loved him and wanted what was best for him. I made my way back to our small hometown. It felt like my whole world was crashing down.

I remember every little detail about that day. It was rainy and damp, which only foreshadowed what was about to come. I confronted him at his house, where he was with his dad, who had recently suffered a stroke. He hadn't gone to school that day because everything was a mess. We went to a small high school, so rumours were flying around everywhere. My circle of friends was broken apart. All I wanted was to talk to him. I wanted the truth. He stood there, withdrawn, without saying a word. I had never seen him like this before. He began to walk away down the street. As he walked away, I said, "That's what you do best; you walk away." Little did I know, in that moment, those would be my last words to him.

I made my way to his neighbour's home, wondering if I should leave his dad unattended, due to the condition he was in. About ten minutes after I arrived, the phone rang and there was word that someone had jumped off the bridge onto Route 95—in the middle of rush hour. I dropped to my knees immediately. I knew. I don't know how, but I knew it was him—the love of my life, my high school sweetheart was gone. He was only seventeen. My life changed forever in that very moment. I was shocked and in disbelief. I was devastated.

The next day, there was a memorial service. After the service was over, I collapsed from emotional exhaustion. My parents had to carry me to the car. I couldn't stop crying. My older brother sat on the bed with me and told me it wasn't my fault what happened. It was hard because I felt guilty and felt a sense of fault in the situation. It took me years to truly know it wasn't my fault.

Up until this point in my life, I had never thought of the word suicide. I didn't know anyone who had committed suicide, nor did I hear much about it through the news. In today's world, I feel like we hear about it every day. I may just have ears for it now, and every time I hear the word suicide, I pay attention. I still constantly wonder how a person's life can be so bad that they resort to suicide. Is it selfish? Some think so. I used to think so. More than sad, I was angry. So angry. He left me to deal with this mess and to deal with it alone.

Guilt. Shock. Anger. Despair. These emotions were triggered for me after his suicide. I experienced all of these emotions bundled up into one. I never knew it was possible to feel so many sensations at one time. And the questions, ugh the questions. They came flying across my head like an annoying screensaver on a computer. What if? How? Why?

All common questions when someone takes their own life. Unfortunately, all common answers, as well. We don't know, and we most likely never will.

Some suicide victims leave behind a note. I do not know if I would have wanted a note. Either way, I didn't have a choice... there was no note. When there is no note left behind, the questions seem more perplexing.

I do know this: what goes on in the depths of someone's soul is only visible to that person. You can think you know a person, but in truth, you can only know as much as they let you. For me, I thought I knew him so well. In the depths of his soul, he was fighting. What he was fighting, I don't know. I do know that he had to be hurting pretty bad to take his own life. No one takes their own life because they are happy in life. It's just not how it works.

Fast forward to present day. It is now thirteen years after the incident. In these thirteen years, I somehow managed to graduate college, earn my master's degree, marry my best friend, and be accepted into massage school. In these thirteen years, I also managed to learn how to fight depression, anxiety, panic... a much greater feat than any education I have ever received.

Moving on—easier said than done, right? It seemed like a constant uphill, never-ending treadmill battle. You want it to end, but it's on a loop and just keeps going. The good news is we are in control of our own treadmills. It took me a long time to figure this out. I went to therapists, psychic mediums, tried new technology, went on pills—you name it, I probably tried it. I wanted someone to fix it. I wanted someone to do the work for me and say it would be OK.

Again, I failed to realize that I was the one in control of my own battle.

As humans, we were born with the gift of choice. Sometimes we choose poorly, other times less poorly, and sometimes we get lucky and choose wisely. However, we are able to judge options and make an educated choice based upon these options. In the aftermath of the suicide of someone you love, you have choices. You play the victim or you play the survivor. I chose poorly at first, but I recovered and changed my choice to a more wise decision. I chose to be a survivor.

I played the victim card for a long time. I, however, was not the victim. He was the victim. I am a survivor. Learning this was a huge step in my journey. You are only the victim if you allow yourself to be. It's that whole "being in charge of your own treadmill" again. Being in control and being able to "stop" it when we want is what makes us survivors. Victims don't have that choice... we do.

I pray that if you are reading this, you have never been through the experience of losing someone you know to suicide. However, if you have, please understand that YOU have a choice. You CAN and WILL survive. We know all too well that life is short. Don't take it for granted. Reach out if you need to. You are in control of your life. Don't let the cobwebs from the past dictate who you are today. Be YOUR best self. Be a survivor.

*Disclaimer: If you or someone you know is struggling with suicide or suicidal thoughts, seek professional help from your local community.

COMPILED by **KRISTY-LEA TRITZ**

Tandy Elisala

Tandy Elisala, MA, CPSC, ACH, CHT, is a certified success coach, mindset mentor, author, and speaker. She is also a certified hypnotherapist, a certified thought-field therapy practitioner, and a Reiki practitioner. Tandy served as VP for one of the largest, private universities in the nation for more than twenty-one years and served as a university faculty member for ten years. She has kicked cancer's butt three times and helps others heal, conquer overwhelm, release what no longer serves them, and gives them powerful and proven strategies to live their lives powerfully and live a life they love. Tandy lives in Tempe, AZ, with her kids, awesome dog, and two cats.

www.tandyelisala.com
tandy@tandyelisala.com
facebook.com/tandyelisala
twitter.com/drtandy
www.youtube.com/tandyelisala
google.com/+tandyelisala
linkedin.com/in/tandye

COMPILED by **KRISTY-LEA TRITZ**

Chapter 29

THIRD TIME'S A CHARM: HOW I KICKED CANCER'S BUTT THREE TIMES

Tandy Elisala

"How quickly can you get here?" was the question from the doctor's office on the other end of the line. I was about to board a plane to return home from a business trip. I was literally walking on the plane when my phone rang. Funny thing was, I had already turned off my phone and felt guided to turn it back on. Ever have those moments? Listen to them!

I had a biopsy the week prior. I knew it couldn't be good news when they wanted me there right away. I had five hours to stew about it on the plane ride home. The next morning, I heard the words, "You have cancer. We need to take you to surgery."

My life changed in an instant. I was a VP for a large university, with a lot of responsibility. Being a single mom and raising my kids virtually alone was challenging. Add their respective school and community commitments and I was one busy mom. I didn't have time for this! With a husband (now ex-husband) more concerned about how busy he was at work, who couldn't be bothered to take me for surgery, I really felt all alone and scared.

Ultimately, my daughter, Amanda, took care of me. She is my rock. She was just eighteen, and I know she was scared for me... for our family: my daughter, Sarah (fourteen), and

COMPILED by KRISTY-LEA TRITZ

my son, Steven (twelve). I knew I had to be strong for them.

You know the saying, you never know how strong you are until being strong is your only choice? Strong was my middle name. I prided myself on constantly "doing" all this stuff and managing it well, thank you very much! Cancer ("c") changed me. Suddenly, things like dishes and laundry didn't matter.

Then, about two years later, this body had another cancer diagnosis. This body had "c" again! Same area of the body. I reflected on my journey thus far and wondered why this was happening. I forged ahead and thankfully caught it early, and recovery was uneventful.

Then, two years later, *another* cancer diagnosis and treatment. Going through cancer once is enough, but THREE times. Really!? I considered myself a positive and a spiritual person, yet this really tested me on all levels. I thought, *Well, things come in threes*. This better be it!

I did a lot to help restore my health and get through this most difficult time in my life. Here are five things I learned along the way that got me through:

1. My Faith

At my core, I knew, felt, and believed I would be okay. I felt this way because I knew my mission in life was to heal and lead others to greatness. I believed I would be okay because I was still fulfilling my mission in life. I also believed I had to be okay for my three kids.

Raising my kids has been the single greatest joy in my life. I had to pull all my strength from deep in my core and do what I needed to do to heal. I accepted that this cancer experience was part of my journey to ultimately help others. I kept this thinking at the forefront of my mind, along with visions of being with my kids at all their important life milestones. This thinking and belief allowed me to plan and live beyond "c."

Never let a diagnosis of any kind define you. Don't take what a doctor says as gospel. Do your own research. Make up your own mind—what you will allow and won't allow in your experience. Recognize you are perfect just the way you are. Have faith that everything will work out as it is supposed to. Having faith and a deep belief in your "why" helps you live your best life now with passion and purpose.

2. Affirmations and the Power of the Mind:

The mind is a very powerful thing! I really, really believe in the power of our minds—to be, do, and have anything we want.

Have you ever heard the term, "What the mind can believe, it can achieve"? I really believe this to be true. What the conscious mind believes sinks into the subconscious mind. Would you rather have more positive thoughts than negative ones? The subconscious mind can't tell the difference between truth and lies. We have tens of thousands of thoughts daily, and it can be extremely difficult to keep all thoughts positive. Making a conscious effort to give yourself kudos or telling yourself "I love you" may sound strange, but it can greatly assist and train your subconscious to have more positive thoughts.

Affirmations are a fabulous way to reach our subconscious mind with thoughts of things we do want.

When this body had cancer, I placed affirmations everywhere! When I say everywhere, I mean everywhere. Doors, cabinets, mirrors, books, cars, computers—anywhere I was, there they were. I wasn't leaving anything to chance! My favorite affirmation during these times was, "My body is in the image and likeness of God, and it is now being restored to perfect health." I had many other affirmations; all related to restored health.

3. Self-Love:

Self-love means honoring yourself and doing what's right for you. It means sometimes saying "NO" to things you are used to saying yes to. It means sleeping in or going to bed early when others in your home are up. It means finding time just for you to do things that keep you connected and grounded with life.

I had to relearn this. I used to say "yes" to everything because I wanted people to like me. I felt I needed to prove myself. I would have no idea if or how this "thing" I said yes to actually fit into my purpose for being here, contributed to my well-being, or was something I actually wanted to do.

Do what feels right for you. If it doesn't fall in line with the above, or your internal guidance system, don't do it.

4. Gratitude:

Gratitude is at the foundation of my belief system. I highly value gratitude and having a gratitude practice was and still is at the heart of it all. I believe gratitude is the foundation to living a life filled with passion, peace, and joy. I was thankful for every little thing that happened.

At my worst, I gave thanks for each breath I took, my legs to walk, my eyes to see, my ears to hear. There is always something to be grateful for. Being in a state of gratitude brings more things in our lives to be grateful for.

One simple way to integrate gratitude into your life is to simply affirm, silently or out loud, three things you are thankful for each morning before getting out of bed. I promise your day will be brighter for it.

5. Appreciate Nature:

Nature is so healing. You don't need to be surrounded by water or mountains to take advantage of the healing power of nature. It can be as simple as spending time outside around trees, the sky, the grass, or whatever is available to you.

One thing I did when first diagnosed with cancer was I went outside and hugged a tree in the backyard. I took deep breaths and imagined being at one with the tree. I visualized all dis*ease* flowing out of my body and into Mother Earth. I lay down on the grass and imagined being surrounded and filled in white and blue healing light. I can't describe the peace I felt spending time with nature. We are all truly one with each other, and nature is a wonderful expression of God. I highly encourage being connected with nature in some way, shape, or form. It's so healing and energizing.

If someone had told me this body would get cancer once, I would have said, no way. But having cancer three times... there is no way I could have prepared for that. I never imagined such a thing. After all, my risk factors were extremely low. There was no "scientific" reason to get cancer. None.

What I've learned is that regardless of what happens in life, it is our responsibility to show up, stand up, and be present. It is our response to situations that dictate the outcome. It is our choice. It is up to us. It always is. I choose faith, power of the mind, affirmations, gratitude, and self-love.

Tara-Lee York

Tara-Lee York loves coffee and WordPress! She is a wife, mother of five, writer, and graphic and web designer. She's passionate about creativity and design. She works with her clients to create brand and web designs that reflect their brand and attract their perfect client. What makes her unique? She takes a piece of her clients' personality and inputs it into their brand designs. She has studied graphic and web design. She is also trained as a life coach and licensed practical nurse. (This means she likes to ask you lots of questions.) She's pretty good at listening, too.

www.inspiredmessagestudio.com
contact@inspiredmessagestudio.com
facebook.com/inspiredmessagestudio
twitter.com/taraleeyork
linkedin.com/in/taraleeyork

COMPILED by **KRISTY-LEA TRITZ**

Chapter 30

REIGNITING MY PASSIONS: SPARKING HOPE FOR THE FUTURE

Tara-Lee York

"You are more powerful than you think!"

The words at the bottom of the e-mail felt as though they were jumping off the page. I stared at the sentence on my screen. My heart embraced the idea, as if it was a life preserver being thrown to me amidst the stormy sea of my emotions.

It was at this moment I chose to believe that I could. No! Not could but *would*! I was going to do this! I was going to run toward my dreams and passions. No matter what that meant or would take.

I was grasping at straws. Everything that I had done seemed to be a failure. I have tried numerous "business opportunities," only for each one to fail. It was my dream to create a business that was unique. My driving force was to have the freedom to be present in my children's lives.

I read these words when I was in the midst of my second diagnosed postpartum depression at thirty-two years old. It was that moment that I chose to take control of my destiny and not look back. I was beginning my journey to finding my voice.

By fifteen, I had watched my mother struggle through the last three of her seven pregnancies. I was her right hand. I watched as morning sickness and high blood pressure took a toll on her body. A week after my youngest sister's birth, Mom suffered a heart attack. As a young woman, my mother's experiences were fresh in my mind. I was not ready for my own journey into motherhood to begin.

At twenty-four and pregnant with my first child, I experienced morning sickness and high blood pressure. When my first son was about ten months old, I was expecting again. I was looking forward to our newest family addition. Things were different this time around. I didn't experience any morning sickness.

When I was nearly six weeks into the pregnancy, I remember jerking forward in my bed. I knew my baby's heart had stopped beating. Five weeks later, I miscarried baby number two. I felt heartbroken. I never realized, before that moment, that you could grieve the death of someone you had never held or seen.

Within the span of four and a half years, I had given birth to four sons. Many days, just caring for them was exhausting. It took all I had to meet their physical needs.

Nights were the darkest. It was then I had the time to reflect on my life. I can still feel the resentment, anger, and hopelessness that had claimed my soul. I had 4 beautiful sons. I should have been happy, but I wasn't. "Your children are healthy. Their father is good to you and them. Your life is secure," I told myself. It didn't matter. I knew something was missing.

Eighteen months after my last son's birth, I finally was given a diagnosis of postpartum. I was miserable, unhappy, and unfulfilled. I found myself drifting further and further away from my family. I wanted to be left alone. I was pushing everyone in my life away. I wanted little or no contact with my children or husband. I felt numb.

In 2011, I found out I was pregnant again—this time with a baby girl! Can you imagine my excitement? It seemed I knew from the moment she was conceived. Her conception and birth seemed to mark the rebirth of my own life. Shortly after she was born, I enrolled in and completed a business, marketing, and life-coaching program.

Throughout the training, I began to dig deep into my soul —doing inner work of letting go of my fears, self-limiting beliefs, and habits that had been holding me hostage. Letting go of my past and embracing the future, I began to reawaken the passions from my youth that had lay dominant.

As a teenager, I remember reading my favourite author, Lucy Maud Montgomery. I wanted to be able to write with freedom and imagination, just as she did. By daring to revisit what had made me fulfilled as a youth, I rediscovered my love for writing, creativity, and designing. I knew I needed a career that would allow me to express my love for all three.

Within a few months, I enrolled in a graphic design, website design, and video editing diploma course. Over the past two years, I have developed new skills that are moving me in a direction that is more aligned with who I really am and what I want to do. Finding true joy in allowing myself to work with my natural strengths and new skills, I have found a career path that is suited for me. I now have marketable skills that will allow me to create a path for myself and will leave me feeling fulfilled. I will be able to affect others' lives in ways that I may not have been able to previously reach.

In my near future, I have plans to write and publish my first book, starting with personal branding. I have come to the realization that we can do, become, and achieve anything we want. All it takes is believing that we can, taking the first steps that propel us forward, and sticking with it even when things get tough. Just remember to take one step at a time. Everything won't happen all at once. It has become my desire to help others connect to their inner soul and create a life and/or business that is aligned with who they are.

In sharing my journey with you, I hope to inspire you to find your own voice, no matter where you are at in your life. Reach through your darkness and pain to claim your future. Giving up is not an option! "You are more powerful than you think!" The world is waiting to hear your message.

In closing, I want to leave you with five actions steps that you can take to help you uncover your passion.

1. Discover your Core

Find what truly matters to you. Take the time to sit down and write a list of things that mean the most in your life. Answer these questions: What do you value? What would you never compromise on? What would you hold onto even though it might cost you everything? Go back through the list until you have narrowed it down to three. You will then have the three things that are at your very core.

2. Embracing What Makes you Different

Your uniqueness, your weaknesses, strengths, skills, and talents are the perfect blend that makes you. Have you ever been teased or ridiculed? Are you afraid of showing the true you because of what people might think? Construct a personal toolkit. Answer these questions: What life and job experience do you have? What are your talents, skills, and strengths you are currently hiding?

3. Leave em' with a Punch

What is the difference that you want to make in this world? In twenty years, when you look back, what regrets do you NOT wish to have? When your time is coming to a close, what would make you look back and say, "I'm leaving them a punch?"

4. Know where you want to go:

Do you have dreams and desires that live deep within your heart? As a child, did you even wonder what you would be become? Perhaps you even pictured it very clearly. As the years and events passed, did you lose sight of that vision? It's possible the reason that you feel discontent and disappointment in your current path is you have lost what you once dreamed was possible.

Before jumping into your future, go back into your past. Was there something you used to love to do that you no longer do? Could you take it up again? What is one thing you could do this week to move you one step closer to that dream?

5. What's Your Why?

This is the reason you do what you do. Your why is what guides your purpose. If you have an understanding of what is your driving force, you are more likely to stand your ground and not give up when reaching your dreams feels tough.

Look within and answer these questions. What do I want to achieve? How do I want to affect those around me? Why is it so important for me to do this? What will happen as result of me failing to do this? What is the driving force that will keep me motivated to reach my dreams and goals?

Ty Will

Ty grew up in Billings, Montana. In 1987, she joined the army. Enlisting in the military was a difficult choice for her but one she is now proud to have made. Ty received the Army Achievement Medal. She wrote her book, *The Female Veteran*, due to the trauma that happened on secret mission.

Ty's goals in hosting the Oscar-nominated documentary, *The Invisible War*, is for people to see the real damage of military sexual trauma, and more important, WHAT THEY CAN DO to stop it. This is an epidemic.

www.thefemaleveteran.com
thefemaleveteran@yahoo.com

COMPILED by **KRISTY-LEA TRITZ**

Chapter 31

LIFE IS A HIGHWAY: A SURVIVOR'S BUMPY ROAD

Ty Will

We have all heard of the analogy that our life is like a highway. We drive around the curves, over mountains, and through the woods to grandma's house.

All kidding aside, our life highway is hard. There is no doubt that some mountains have snow-packed roads, forcing us to slow down. Other times, there's that moment when going 85 mph—top down, 100 degrees outside, and your hair whipping in the wind—just to get to the lake is all you care about.

As we contemplate the importance of our life, I sit back and wonder... does anyone see the cars on that highway?

Take a moment and look at the car next to you. Is the vehicle new and shiny? Is the vehicle old and rusty, possibly a few dents? What about those cool old classics? We all love seeing those babies come down the road. Nothing like turning your head and saying, "Did you see that car?" Then you both start talking about that car. What year? What colour? Was it the true colour? Do you think it's all original? All of a sudden the mood changes in your car. That is the moment where everyone is happy and life is good.

In my life's highway I feel like a 1966 Chevy Nova—classic muscle car. Vroom, vroom, baby. I feel the seat rumbling under my butt right now! I was born in 1966, and the world was in turmoil but my car shined and so did I.

Childhood seemed normal to me. I had brothers and a twin sister. We were not rich, but we had food every night and a roof over our heads.

So I guess you can say that my 1966 Chevy Nova was gassed, and the oil was changed frequently.

It's weird to think that our lives are a highway, going over this bump and that hill, but what happens when we get a flat tire?

My shiny new car got a flat when I was a teenager. I was married young, I had two babies and was divorced twice by the time I was twenty. I quickly changed the flat tire in my life and carried on.

Watching a TV commercial, I heard the words, "We will pay for college. All you have to do is join the army. Be all you can be!" It clicked. I felt the engine revving up the seat to my 1966 Chevy Nova... and so was my future.

My parents looked after my children while I was in boot camp and advance individual training (AIT). I was going to be an operating room specialist. I loved that job. It was fun and exciting. This job would benefit as a career after the army. This 1966 Chevy Nova just got a wax job, and she looked great!

As with any great wax job, my 1966 Chevy Nova got dull. I wore out and decided to change careers to satellite communications. I coded and decoded messages. I went on active duty in 1989.

The new unit I drove into was nothing more than

spectacular! Talk about cool vehicles—the unit was like James Bond. It came with all the gadgets of a 007 car—and secret missions. Satellite communications at that time was one of the most important factors for the military.

Out of nowhere, my 1966 Chevy Nova had head-on collision. This collision was the sergeant. I'm not sure what kind of car he drove, because I never saw it coming.

I felt safe in the army. In 1990, our unit was deployed to Desert Storm. The sergeant and I were part of the team that stayed behind to support those who were deployed. The real reason I had to stay behind was that I was female! The commander was a sexist pig, and not one female was deployed with the unit.

Sergeant began harassing me. I couldn't roll the wire up right. I couldn't start and stop the two types of generators according to "his ways." There was one occasion when the sergeant made me start and stop them for five hours straight, with temperatures in the lower teens. My fingers were so frostbitten. To this day, my fingers are still sensitive.

I have never been in a head-on collision with a vehicle in real life. I can only imagine how scary it must be. My life's highway collision was being raped by the sergeant.

The sergeant and I were sent on a secret mission. He now added sexual harassment to his list of torments. At the hotel we were staying at, he put me on parade rest—a military term meaning he put me at attention—and proceeded to make fun of my body and degrade me in front of the civilians surrounding the pool.

I called back to the unit and asked for help. NO ONE CAME. I was raped the following week by the sergeant. He threatened to kill me and kill and rape my daughter. I called back to the unit again. Still NO HELP CAME. No medics, no helicopters. NO ONE came TO SAVE ME.

I was now sitting on the side of the highway; my 1966 Chevy Nova unrecognizable. The tow truck picked me up and dropped me off in my garage.

I sat in the garage for a very long time—twenty-two years. My tires got flat, the engine froze up, rust took over, the layer of dust was overwhelming. Life's highway kept on moving.

I have finally accepted life is OK. But... is life really just OK? Can you believe life is spectacular again? Of course you can!

One day, someone walked into my garage. He opened the doors wide and the sun shone on that 1966 Chevy Nova. There was even a hint of glitter on the metal. He saw the beauty that once was and started fixing that 1966 Chevy Nova. It was hard at first. The engine kept freezing up, didn't want to budge—it was stubborn. He kept working on the engine. Then one day it turned over. That man was Jesus Christ. He showed me what real love was and gave me hope again.

How wonderful it was to feel the sun's rays on my face, the water on my lips, and the grass under my toes.

I survived! I am still here and so is that 1966 Chevy Nova —with a nice new shiny paint job. This last paint job required help.

The help came because of the documentary, *The Invisible War*. What a dirty little secret our military is hiding. This documentary brought it to light.

I can talk about the rape and trauma now. It was time. I sat down and wrote the book, *The Female Veteran*. I knew I had to write this book. I thought it was time to shed light on military sexual trauma and the aftermath the women survivors live.

I heard one day on TV about Senator Kristin Gillibrand of New York trying to pass the Military Justice Improvement Act. I couldn't believe it! Our voices are now being heard. I sent her a copy of my book. What I got in return was priceless.

I expressed on the back cover of the book that I never received my medal from that secret mission I was on. I got a letter from Senator Gillibrand requesting paperwork proof of the secret mission and the medal I was supposed to receive.

Two months later, on October 8, 2013, my medal came in the mail. I was validated! Senator Kristin Gillibrand cared enough about little old me out in Timbuktu, Wyoming. Thank you, Senator!

My 1966 Chevy Nova is on the road again. Vroom, vroom. I feel the seat rumbling under my butt again. You know what? It feels great! I have a direction now; I am starting my new business making T-shirts for female veterans— something for the girls now.

I am proud of my service to my country, but what I'm most proud of is what I am doing now—starting my motivational speaking career to inform society that rape in the military or in the civilian world must stop.

Our voices, our pens, our minds, our lives, and the transformation of the way we accomplish this epic challenge will come from persistence!

Persistence is to never let this happen again! Persistence is to never be ashamed of talking about rape!

My life's highway and that classic muscle car, a 1966 Chevy Nova, have been made new again. There is sun shining on the road ahead, and I am noticing people turning their heads to see this shiny classic.

The importance of noticing the other cars on the highway of life is to never give up on that classic sitting in the garage. Love is our hope for these classics. If we care enough, love enough, and never give up, the sun will shine on the classic car and that will be the start of their new journey on this life's highway.

Vanessa Higgins

Vanessa is a water conservation educator in Alberta, Canada. Her dream has always been to connect people with the importance of the natural world and to understand the connection between its health and our quality of life. Growing up in the Edmonton River Valley, Vanessa developed a strong connection to the waters that bring the city to life. Following a depressive episode after her divorce, Vanessa found healing in an online blog, where she shared nature's daily inspirations for her readers, in an effort to pull herself away from debilitating thoughts and emotions.

www.inspirevanessa.blogspot.com

COMPILED by **KRISTY-LEA TRITZ**

Chapter 32

NORTHERN LIGHT SPECIAL: OVERCOMING BURN OUT

Vanessa Higgins

Leaves, trees, and clouds were my escape as a young child. I liked to call it my sacred space. I felt interconnected with the earth, to life, to infinite love.

I experienced the traumas of sexual abuse by my uncle and brother, whom I loved deeply throughout much of my elementary school days. My uncle would tell me how disgusting and dirty I was and that no one would ever love me if I told. The pressure to gain acceptance from others began to creep into my life. Maybe this is the place where I began taking on too much, and my process of burnout started to take shape.

My young life forever changed on my Grade 4 trip to the landfill with Ms. Bennett. My yellow bus was slowly chugging up the side of a mountain made of human discards and trash. When I stepped onto the wasted Earth, I looked down at the majestic North Saskatchewan River Valley. I was so scared that leachate from the landfill might enter the source of so many communities' drinking water. I felt a calling. It was up to me. I must help protect Mother Earth and protect my sacred spaces and the sacred spaces for future generations.

My friend Angela and I began an environmental club at school. We collected pop bottles and raised money to save acres of Brazilian rainforest. I felt like I was being defeated because I couldn't save it all. We did lunchtime viewings of *Fern Gully* to raise awareness of the complicated environmental issues facing our rivers and forests. We may have only reached a few interested students, but we felt as powerful as Captain Planet and the Planeteers™

My passions fuelled my life—marine biology club in high school, environmental sciences in post-secondary, and a consulting job testing water and air after graduation. It was just not enough. I wanted to do more.

I eagerly added challenges to my plate. My bosses would have meetings with me, trying to take tasks away and refocus my energy. I fought to hang on because I knew that the impact would end without my hands doing the work—which left me feeling alone and isolated.

Finally, my director took me aside and said, "Vanessa, you have two fires to fuel—your work fire and your personal fire. Your work fire is a bonfire; it's strong and can sustain itself for a while. You need to focus your energy on your personal fire or you're going to burn out."

Burn out is exactly what I did. I lost touch with reality. I lost my husband. I lost it all! I began hallucinating a bloody scene and I called 9-1-1. I didn't know my name, I thought my husband had died during his tour in Afghanistan, and I thought I had murdered all my friends and family. That was the worst day of my life. None of this was true but the doctors and nurses understood my stress and took very good care of me.

I fell into a deep depression after my manic episode—for nearly three years. I couldn't shower, eat, or talk to loved ones. It felt like I was dragging around the corpse of my former self and the load was getting heavier with every step. Suicide was on my mind every day. I felt that I didn't deserve to be among the other creatures on planet Earth. I felt worthless and stupid. Even my passion for the environment had been snuffed out... there was no hope.

My bosses never gave up on me. My corpse hadn't come back to life yet—I was still living in a deep, dark state. However, my support system encouraged me to keep on moving one step in front of the other, so I tried to live a "normal" life. I had never felt more alone.

Larry, my neighbour, noticed my weight loss. He congratulated my success. I shared that I just simply wasn't eating. He said I was depressed, and that I needed to help another person. Yeah, right! Where would I get the energy and focus? He didn't know that I hadn't even taken a shower all week. But I decided to take my aunt swimming. She has trouble walking and the water sets her free from her limitations. I watched her face twist up into a look of ecstasy and gratitude. I realized, hey, I did that! I matter. I *did* deserve to be on the planet. Poetically, you could say that I spent my career saving water, and now water was saving me. I always get emotional saying that.

After several years of group therapy, weekly psychologist visits, bi-weekly psychiatrist meetings, med changes, a work coach, and time off through disability insurance, I have finally found her. I did yoga in the healing garden, I created goal collages, and I put on singing performances. I was really coming alive! No illness was going to get the best of me!

When I was in the hospital, I prayed to God every day that he would return me to myself. It took a lot of twists and turns, but from a distance, honestly, the journey was beautiful.

Taking my aunt swimming also brought me to these powerful superwomen and this book. In the spring of 2014, I met my mentor, Kristy-Lea, at the local recreation center. Our souls began a dance that will transform into a lasting support system. I cannot send enough loving kindness out to all those amazing people who guided and lifted me up through the darkest years of my existence. You all know who you are, my sweet angels. You allowed this butterfly to soar.

Tips of Transformation

I could write a whole book on all the creative ways I used love, art and supports to transport me to a better place and a perfect—yet flawed and unique—me.

1.   Try to channel your emotion through writing—in a blog or a gratitude journal, or perhaps sharing your story with respectful listeners.

2.   Get your mind onto paper, visually. Charcoal, markers, paint, photography, scrapbook, and collage material can help you express your love, your needs, and your journey.

3.   Mindfulness on the road–When I see a white truck, I say a positive mantra about my job, and when I see a black truck I say, "I am amazing." Saying those positive affirmations sprinkles sweet sugar onto your mind. Could you do this with people walking, or each time your dog goes for a pee? Think of a frequent, meditative option that works

best for your wellbeing.

4. Yoga–It's not for everyone, but there is something loving about paying direct attention to your breath and the small movements of your miraculous body. It is a celebration of self, a surrender to love. My yoga teacher always told us, "Know that whatever you did today, you did enough." You are good enough as you are, you are perfect as you are. You may be far away from your goals, but this is where your journey has placed you, for better or for worse. You are enough.

5. Performance–Performance is a powerful tool to manage depression. It reminds you that you have unique movement, sound, and storytelling abilities that must be shared with the world. Create a playlist of inspirational songs to get you up, get you moving, or get you singing in the car. Try to find a spiritual dance therapy—where you breathe, celebrate, and focus on different parts of your emotional body. A dance teacher once told me that emotions are just energy in motion.

I like to tell my friends to be like the Northern Lights. Don't try to be a rock star who shines so bright and so long that she burns herself out. That is unnecessary and can often be unhealthy in many different manifestations.

Instead, come out and shine your light, take a risk, and paddle toward your goals, remembering to take time to retreat and recover. Crawl into your cocoon with a good book, a glass of wine, and a laugh or two with friends. Once you recharge your soul, it is safe to come out and shine again with a new project and a renewed hope. The light in me sees the Northern Lights in you.

COMPILED by **KRISTY-LEA TRITZ**

The Next Step Forward

"Change is best embraced with the mentality of first I crawl, then I walk, then I leap. It takes one step in front of the other, one choice at a time, to create change." ~Kristy-Lea Tritz

The journey through this book has come to an end. You started at the beginning and made your way through to the end page. Really, when it comes to this book, it has no end. Here is why: The lives of those who shared with you continue to go on. They continue to move forward in their choices to live life to the fullest.

Here you are, as you read these words, wanting a life of change. You want a life where you can feel that freedom from within to express who you really are. You want to live healthy and happy from the inside out.

The one thing each one of these authors had is support. One of the most important things in life as you move from where you are to where you want to be is support. The kind of support that listens before it speaks, that loves instead of judges!

Your story may have been echoed in the lives you read about in this book—maybe you feel trapped, unloved, unwanted, imprisoned, or lonely. Possibly you're in a relationship that is unhealthy. Maybe you have lost all sense of who you are as an individual, or maybe you are at a point where you recognize something has to change. Oftentimes, when in the throes of emotion or circumstance, you can lose sight of what needs to be the first step in the process of change. Most times, that step is deciding for yourself that you need to change.

Change really does not begin with a "you"—meaning others; it begins with an "I"—meaning yourself. The work I have and currently do with women and couples brings that spark of life back! There is nothing greater than witnessing the change of a woman—one who cries herself to sleep because of the pain she lives daily—and seeing her blossom into a woman who knows who she is, what she wants, and then goes after it.

Are you ready to take that next step forward in your life? Are you ready to get to the heart of the matter and find peace in your life, have a relationship where you feel valued and loved for *you*, and move from that place of overwhelm to a place where you are healthy heart, mind, body, and soul? Let's journey together because YOUR HEART MATTERS!

If you are in a place in your life where you would like to see your story in print or maybe you would like to do your own compilation book with others please connect with me at contact@empowerandinspirepublishing.com

With much joy for the future,

Kristy-Lea Tritz

kristyleatritz@gettotheheartofthematter.ca- Email

www.supwerwomanmyths.com - Book/Summit/Program

www.empowerandinspirepublishing.com - Publishing Info

www.gettotheheartofthematter.ca - Coaching/Programs

www.kristyleatritz.com - Personal Site

www.yourheartmatters.ca - Podcast Site

Praise for Kristy-Lea Tritz

Kim Boudreau Smith

I met Kristy-Lea in 2013, where I spent a quick moment on a mutual project with her—our relationship has been growing and evolving ever since. It is an honour to be a part of this project that Kristy-Lea is leading. She stands for women's voices, and Kristy-Lea has been evolving her voice since the onset of this book. I believe we must walk our talk, and Kristy-Lea does just that. She has strengthened her voice to be a stronger woman for her clients, and most importantly, herself. She is authentic and passionate, while wearing her heart on her sleeve, as she supports others to step into their courage, strength, and power through their voice. This is one woman whose kindness you don't want to mistake for a weakness. Her intuition and brilliance can lead women to their clarity and go on after dealing with pain, loss, and adversity. She gets it! She is there for the support, guidance, and offers her experience as you transition, transform, and become more confident through your voice.

Kristy-Lea, you have brought together a beautiful group of co- authors. You so deserve this published book and the lives you and your co-authors will change, inspire, grow, and even shed some tears. You are a poised, giving, and a very loving woman. Every person that reads *SUPERWOMAN MTYHS: Break The Silence And Speak Up Your Truth*—you will touch their heart. That is just what you do, every day.

Kim M Smith

Kim Boudreau Smith, Inc. Proprietor, Bold Radio Station (www.boldradiostation.com)

Mary Knebel

I met Kristy-Lea entirely by chance. I had recently begun using Facebook to promote my coaching business and thought it would be a good idea to meet other fellow coaches doing similar things. I saw Kristy-Lea's Facebook profile picture in a group we were both in, and I thought to myself, "She looks friendly!" I reached out to her, but because I had just started using Facebook, I hadn't really developed my profile yet and she thought I was spamming her. I assured her I was not, and I'm so grateful that she trusted I wasn't a psycho Internet stalker!

Kristy-Lea's coaching business is called Get to the Heart of the Matter. She's a heart-centered women's empowerment coach, and it's easy to see why. Kristy-Lea wants every woman to feel like she is living a life that truly fills her heart up—where she is heard, empowered, and able to be the biggest and best version of herself. Kristy-Lea is sensitive, compassionate, and sees what's possible for every woman she meets. But she also gets that women are often vulnerable and struggling and need help, and that's where she comes in. She helps women heal their hearts, so that they no longer feel so alone, scared, or not living on-purpose.

During the course of getting to know her, Kristy-Lea asked me to co-host her weekly radio show, *A Woman's Voice*, which I was honoured to do several times. Again, Kristy-Lea believes that every woman should have a chance to let her voice be heard so that she can live a life that ignites her heart. We talked about a variety of subjects on each of the radio shows, and the hour always flew by! Kristy-Lea always came to the shows armed with several questions that would help the women who were listening get the most out of the topic at-hand. Kristy-Lea is one of those people who really cares and really wants to help.

She and I have evolved and grown our businesses together, and during the course of all of this, we have become great friends. Even though we've never met in person (we don't even live in the same country!), we are always there to lend each other words of support and encouragement along the way. I know that Kristy-Lea is truly a heart-centered coach and always leads from her heart. She sees the best in others and believes that every woman should have a chance to have a life they love and that lights them up. She is a fighter for all women and gives them a voice, even when they don't have one. Above all, Kristy-Lea is a dreamer and a visionary and is not scared to go after what she wants. Not only will this ensure that she goes far, but she's serving as an inspiration for women everywhere who have big dreams and are ready to get everything their heart desires.

Mary Knebel

Certified money breakthrough coach and money intuitive founder of www.Moneypreneurs.com

"*Everything in life is a labour of LOVE, but the only way to LIVE, is to LIVE truly immersed in a life of LOVE!*

~Kristy-Lea Tritz